Coaching for the Future: How smart companies use coaching and mentoring

D1450683

Janice Caplan studied Italian and French prior to moving into the HR field, initially with Alitalia and then International Harvester Inc. Her career took her into the City of London with Midland Montagu, where, after a period responsible for recruitment and general personnel operations, she became Head of Training and Development.

Her work in personnel development and the alignment of HR with corporate strategy led her to co-found Scala Associates. This consultancy has advised a wide range of City, industrial and commercial firms. In more recent years she and her partners have been active in leadership, executive coaching and HR strategy programmes, using the latest technology to deliver employee opinion surveys and 360-degree assessments through their website and online questionnaires.

Janice's interest in coaching originated through her studies in organisational psychology for an MA in Human Resources. Her continuing commitment to helping individuals and organisations achieve their potential and manage change has led her to act as mentor and executive coach on people issues to directors and senior managers. Janice is an associate of the CESMA business school in Milan and through them has access to a European coaching network.

A past chairman of the Institute of Personnel Management's Central London Group and committee member of its North London Branch, Janice is currently a member of the CIPD's training and development advisory panel and course leader of their Strategies in Recruitment and Selection training programme.

Although Janice has written a number of articles for management journals, this is her first book.

The Chartered Institute of Personnel and Development is the leading publisher of books and reports for personnel and training professionals, students, and for all those concerned with the effective management and development of people at work. For details of all our titles, please contact the Publishing Department:

tel. 020–8263 3387
fax 020–8263 3850
e-mail publish@cipd.co.uk
The catalogue of all CIPD titles can be viewed on the CIPD website:
www.cipd.co.uk/bookstore

Coaching for the Future

How smart companies use coaching and mentoring

Janice Caplan

Chartered Institute of Personnel and Development

Published by the Chartered Institute of Personnel and Development,
CIPD House, Camp Road, London, SW19 4UX

First published 2003
Reprinted 2004

Design by Beacon GDT, Mitcheldean, Gloucestershire
Typesetting by Fakenham Photosetting Ltd, Fakenham, Norfolk
Printed in Great Britain by The Cromwell Press, Trowbridge, Wiltshire

Front cover image photographed by Guus Rijven, www.neilwilkin.com

British Library Cataloguing in Publication Data
A catalogue record for this book is available from the British Library

ISBN 0–85292–958–7

The views expressed in this book are the author's own and
may not necessarily reflect those of the CIPD.

Chartered Institute of Personnel and Development, CIPD House,
Camp Road, London SW19 4UX
Tel: 020 8971 9000   Fax: 020 8263 3333
E-mail: cipd@cipd.co.uk Website: www.cipd.co.uk
Incorporated by Royal Charter. Registered Charity No. 1079797.

Acknowledgements

The discussions, research and writing that created this book spanned almost 12 months. During that time, many organisations and individuals have been exceptionally generous with their time, experience and insights. My family have been extremely supportive; my son, Mark Finch, came up with the title of this book and my husband, Brian Finch, reviewed my writing and helped me think through many ideas.

I have a special debt of gratitude to:

Assa Ephraty, Vice-President of Research and Development, Millimetrix Broadband Networks, Tel Aviv

and

Fiona Hall, independent coach and formerly Customer Services Coach, Prudential

who were enormously generous with their time, reading, rereading, reviewing and commenting on several chapters of this book, Assa Ephraty from an international line manager's viewpoint and Fiona Hall from that of a professionally qualified and experienced coach.

This book benefits greatly from the detailed case studies and observations that have been given to me by:

John Bailey, Director of Coaching, KPMG
Justine Campbell-Marsh, Ernst & Young
Mike Laws, Learning and Development Manager, Ernst & Young
Moira Siddons, Consultant, PricewaterhouseCoopers
Ian Canning, Head of Human Resources, Zurich London
Stephen Liggins, corporate banker, New York
Fiona Anderson, Assignment Editor, Newsgathering, BBC News
Carla Hargis, Talent Coach, Newsgathering, BBC News
Joanne Smith, Call Centre Manager, Prudential
Julia Blandford, Project Manager, Deutsche Bank
Sean Moran, Director, Customer Delivery, Barclaycard Merchant Services
Jodi Myers, Director of Performing Arts, Royal Festival Hall
Pam Henderson, Director, Arts Marketing Association
Anita Traynor, People Manager, eBusiness services, BTexact Technologies
Mandy Messenger, Consultant, Leadership Dynamics, Executive Resourcing & Development, British Telecom
Robert Briggs, Senior Management, University for Lloyds TSB
Angie Charles, HR Manager, Career Management, University for Lloyds TSB
Liz Davis, Head of Workforce Development Division, Cabinet Office
Antonella d'Apruzzo, Training and Job Orientation Manager, Sfera S.p.A. of Enel Corporation S.p.A., Italy
Neil Hoskings, CEO, 360 Financial Training

Mark Prime, Senior Consultant, Training & Development, Citigroup Corporate and Investment Banking, Europe

Sue Kingman, Vice President, Citigroup

Katy Roberts, HR Generalist, Citigroup

Anne McPaul, Vice President, Citigroup

Janet Hayes, PricewaterhouseCoopers

Julia Eadie, the Cabinet Office, now Department of Health

This book similarly benefits from the specialist help, experience and advice so generously given by:

Martyn Sloman, CIPD Adviser: Learning, Training and Development

Elio Vera, Director, CESMA Business School, Milan and Vice President, European Training and Development Federation

Eric Parsloe, Director of Oxford School of Coaching and Mentoring, Trustee and Board Member of the European Mentoring and Coaching Council

Debbie Kingsley, Director, TMPL Consultants/Training

Alex Wise, Director, Loud and Clear Public Relations

Steve Roche, Professional Coach and Trainer

Michael E. Travis, Principal, LeadPerformance, Executive Development Services, USA

Anthony Jackson, Regional Training Director, American Life Insurance Company

Doug King, Strategy Consultant, HR Excellence

Louis Searchwell, Project Research Officer, University of Wales, Bangor

Jo Ayoubi, Director, Smartstaff

Professor Bob Garratt, Executive Coach and Director, Board Performance Ltd

Sally Garratt, Executive Coach and Director, Board Performance Ltd

Simone Emmett, Executive Coach, Strategic Awareness

Louise Sheppard, Executive Coach

Robert Craven, Managing Director, The Directors' Centre

Ros Taylor, Executive Coach, Psychologist and Broadcaster

Glenda Stone, CEO, Aurora GCM Limited

Jessica Rolph, CIPD Adviser: Learning, Training and Development

Kim Coe, CEO, Askhow2.com

Professor Barry D. Cookson, Laboratory of Hospital Infection, Public Health Laboratory Service and Birkbeck University

Haley Lawrence, Inspirational Coaching International, Business and Life Coach

Maxine Klein, Trainer/Psychologist, Maxiskills

I am also immensely grateful to the following people who allowed me access to their research:

Silvia Guarnieri, graduate in training and development processes, Milan

Elizabeth Marks, Accomplish

Georgina Woudstra, Impact Coaching

Finally, thanks to those who gave additional information on practices in Europe:

Sandra Ottolenghi, Partner, Mida S.p.A., Milan; Philippe Rosinski, Belgium;

Sissel Stoltenberg, Norway; Hannes, Evz Coaching, Germany; Helio Moreira, Portugal.

Contents

Preface

This book is written in the context of significant changes that have occurred and are occurring in the ways we do business and the ways organisations work – often termed 'The New Economy' or 'The Knowledge-based Economy' or, indeed, 'The Connected Economy'. These changes affect all organisations: commercial, not-for-profit and government agencies. Brought on by globalisation, significant improvements in technology and the increasing sophistication of consumers, these changes have created a business model that owes far more to controlling and utilising information, knowledge and intangible assets than to managing physical machinery and tangible assets. With this new business model, managing the knowledge embedded in the organisation, ensuring the continuous development of that knowledge and managing the knowledge worker are critical to competitive success. Possibly the most powerful single technique for achieving these aims is the use of coaching.

Coaching is about enhancing and developing the performance of the individual. It is about enabling them to cope with managing change, business transformation, restructuring, growth and technological development. This has a direct impact on the performance of the business. The value of coaching is that it is a way of learning that is highly personal, flexible and individualised. It can be tailored at one and the same time to the needs of the individual and the needs of the organisation. It is about investing in the individual. It is also a technique and a leadership style that suits the independent-minded, innovative 'knowledge' worker, leading to increased commitment, productivity and satisfaction.

Recent surveys bear testimony to the success of coaching for the business and the individual. A Fortune 500 firm and Pyramid Resource Group, a coaching services company in the US, engaged MetrixGlobal LLC[1] to determine the business benefits and return on investment for an executive coaching programme. This survey found that coaching produced a 529 per cent return on investment and significant intangible benefits to the business. Sixty per cent of the respondents were able to identify specific financial benefits that came as a result of their coaching. Overall, productivity and employee satisfaction were cited as the areas most significantly affected by the coaching.

Similar results were revealed in a survey by Manchester Inc,[2] which studied 100 executives from Fortune 1000 companies. The Manchester Inc survey found that 'a company's investment in providing coaching to its executives realised an average return on investment of almost six times the cost of coaching'. The study also established that companies that provided coaching achieved 'improvements in productivity, quality, organisational strength, customer service and shareholder value. They received fewer customer complaints and were more likely to retain executives who had been coached.'

A defining characteristic of coaching is that it is a one-to-one learning process. There is a coach, who may be a more senior executive, an outside consultant or a peer within an organisation, and there is a learner. Generally the relationship involves an encouragement for the learner to discuss issues and identify problems and solutions for themselves, with a minimum of direction. However, the process can cover a wide range of uses and techniques, and this whole spectrum will be discussed in this book.

Coaching techniques may be used by a manager to develop more junior staff. But they may also be used at any level within organisations, right up to the department head or chief executive. Executive coaching is commonly arranged for senior people: to keep up with change, to reinvigorate a business or to support executives when they have been promoted, especially when this is to a more strategic role, perhaps with people management or strategic responsibilities for the first time.

Coaching can be a liberating stimulus to strategic ideas for the top executive, whose status would be damaged by throwing out mad ideas among colleagues in the hope that one in a hundred was a winner. It often fills a gap in personal development and provides a sounding board for senior people who may not have anyone within their organisations with whom to discuss certain management issues.

Coaching is also used to support training. Studies show that as few as 8 to 12 per cent of those who attend training translate new skills into measurable performance improvement.[3] The principal cause of this failure lies in the lack of follow-up, reinforcement or support: the trainee goes 'off site', learns, and then returns to the day-to-day pressures of their role where they often find it hard to apply what they have learnt. It has been shown that the effectiveness of training is significantly enhanced when it is followed up and supported by coaching.

Many writers and academics draw distinctions between coaching and mentoring, sometimes assigning different techniques to each. I believe these distinctions confuse. Mostly, this book will speak of coaching and mentoring interchangeably and will use 'coaching' as a composite term. I will also refer to the person being coached as the learner. I see coaching as a process involving two people, where the aim is for one of them to learn something new, or develop their skills and knowledge in some way. The process embraces a range of aims, models and techniques, and the critical factor is to match those employed by the coach to the learner's needs.

The frenetic development of technologies is opening up new and exciting possibilities for the effective delivery of learning. Much of the future development of coaching may come from harnessing these new technologies and exploiting the possibilities of delivery online. In this book, e-learning and the potential of online coaching are explored in some depth.

This book is directed primarily at those with responsibilities for human resource management in organisations but is also likely to be of interest to line managers. It sets out the many different ways that coaching can be used as a strategic solution for business issues, as well as how it can help individuals with their personal and career development. Part One of the book is constructed as an anthology, bringing under one cover many examples of excellence and innovation in the field. I have been influenced by the people I have met in carrying out this research and hope this may serve some part in encouraging coaching into the mainstream of people management, if the reader is similarly inspired. I also hope that it will add fuel to the debate on the need to professionalise coaching.

In looking at coaching as a strategic solution, I seek to give extensive, practical guidance to human resource practitioners to enable them to introduce such ideas into their own organisations, or to help build on initiatives already in place.

In Part Two, 'Managing the Coaching Process', I seek to assist personnel practitioners with the logistics of arranging and managing the coaching process. I put forward ideas on how to work with colleagues to help them choose appropriate learning solutions, identify learning needs, choose an external coach, contract with the coach, manage relationships and evaluate success. I also set out the main skills and techniques of being a coach and look at how HR professionals can themselves use coaching techniques in their day-to-day dealings with their line colleagues. My aim here is to enable HR practitioners to understand the coaching process and manage it. I am not attempting to explain how to be a coach. There are many other books that already do this, and I refer in a bibliography to those that have helped me.

Over the past year of writing this book, I have been to numerous networking events and meetings and have spoken to a large number of people in organisations. Many people have confessed that they do not understand what coaching is about. This is unsurprising, as coaching is relatively new and its possibilities are still being explored.

I hope this book will add clarity. I believe clarity is important if coaching is to continue to evolve. I hope to offer people ideas that they can implement, but I also hope to raise levels of awareness and thinking, and give people the language and information that will enable them to promote coaching initiatives to their boards and business colleagues. By adding clarity, I hope to help coaches develop themselves, find their niches and work out how best to position themselves in the market. So while this book looks at everything from the point of view of the personnel practitioner, it will also, hopefully, be invaluable to anyone who is or wishes to be a coach.

To obtain the material for this book I conducted interviews with nearly 60 people from over 20 different businesses and 10 coaching organisations. I am grateful to each and every collaborator, all of whom have been very helpful. I have tried to steer a path between attributing comments and material but not advertising or promoting any individual or business that is selling services. I hope I have managed to do justice to all contributors.

This book is not a formal research project. The way I have selected the material and organisations for this book is based on my own judgement. I have carried out much book and Internet research. In so doing, I have studied the works of the leaders in the field and many others. I have contacted numerous organisations and people and have selected initiatives which I find of special interest and which illustrate a particular strategic solution.

This does not mean that there are not other uses for coaching or that I have covered every possible angle. It is that I have exercised judgement and made a choice for the reader. In writing this book and selecting material, I have also drawn extensively on my own background as a personnel practitioner, a personnel consultant and a specialist coach.

NOTES AND REFERENCES

1   ANDERSON M. C. (2001) *Executive Briefing: Case study on the return on investment of executive coaching*. Iowa USA, MetrixGlobal. 2 November. www.metrixglobal.net.

2   See www.manchesterusa.com

3   SKIFFINGTON S. Dr. *and* ZEUS P. (1999) 'What is Executive Coaching?' *Management Today*. November.

Part One

Coaching as a strategic solution

What exactly is coaching? The question has been asked of me countless times by HR and business people. It has even been asked by people who have sat through a conference or a series of presentations on the very subject. Yet no one ever asked me that question when I said I was having tennis coaching. Why is it so difficult to understand the concept of coaching connected with work when it is apparently easy in the context of sport?

Even more astonishing is that many people who are themselves coaches, or who use coaches, fail to understand the full range of possibilities that coaching can cover. The most common are the people who say, 'We don't do any coaching here', but then, on further questioning, it turns out they run a highly effective mentoring programme.

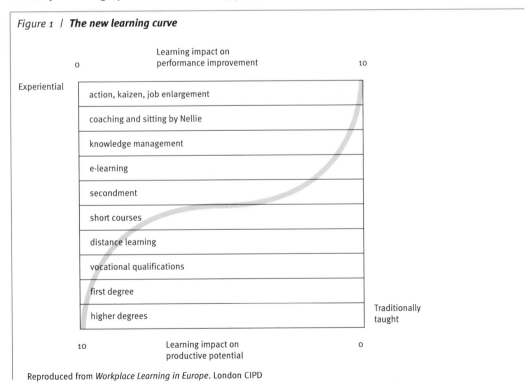

Figure 1 | *The new learning curve*

Reproduced from *Workplace Learning in Europe*. London CIPD

I do not believe that the confusion comes from lack of understanding about what coaching is. Rather, I believe it arises from a lack of understanding about what coaching can achieve. It is not necessary to ask what tennis coaching is because everyone knows instantly that it is to help me improve my game of tennis through one-to-one tuition, exercises and encouragement that develop my skills and my confidence. What we find difficult is to make the link that just such development can be achieved in behaviour and in a wide variety of non-physical skills. We tend to think we are what we are, rather than that a poor listener, for example, can become a good listener through a little effort and some skilled coaching assistance.

We tend to accept we can change our knowledge base through reading or classroom learning but ignore the ability to change our softer skills such as communication, public speaking, leading a team or formulating strategy. These are not genetically determined characteristics – they are learnt and therefore skills capable of improvment. Even knowledge can be improved through coaching, as discussed later in this book.

It is estimated that coaching and mentoring are the third most frequently used solutions to learning in UK organisations, behind on-the-job training and the traditional training course.[1] This represents a considerable investment. My aim in the first part of this book is to help businesses maximise this investment. My main theme here is that the best results are achieved when coaching is closely aligned with business strategy.

Increasingly, people are recognising that learning agility is one of the most important criteria for senior leadership. Knowing we should be learning is easy. The difficulty is to know if we are learning the right things. This represents my second theme, which is that coaching is a highly effective way of helping people know what to learn and how to do it.

NOTES AND REFERENCES

1   CHARTERED INSTITUTE OF PERSONNEL AND DEVELOPMENT *Workplace Learning in Europe*. London, CIPD. Available at: http://www.cipd.co.uk/infosource/conference.asp

2   PARSLOE E. *and* WRAY M. (2000) *Coaching and Mentoring: Practical methods to improve learning*. London, Kogan Page.

1

Coaching as an organisational culture

Today's business environment is characterised by a number of conditions that are driving organisations towards a coaching culture. These drivers include the need for knowledge management; the changes that have occurred in the psychological contract and the expectations people have about work; ever-increasing competition; and growing appreciation in larger companies that they need to plan for succession and develop their own leaders. These drivers are affecting organisations across all sectors. They have had a particular impact on professional services firms and have been key influencers on the development of a coaching culture in the three major international accounting firms – KPMG, Ernst & Young and PwC – featured in this chapter.

In examining what a coaching culture is and how it can be developed, there are many questions to be considered: What is organisational culture? What is a coaching culture? What drives the change to a coaching culture? How do you change the culture of an organisation? What business imperatives does such a culture address?

Moreover, the culture of an organisation is reinforced and underpinned by leadership styles and management processes that encourage the desired values and behaviours. What are the leadership styles of a coaching organisation? What are the key management processes of a coaching organisation? How can an organisation go about developing a coaching culture? Can my organisation develop such a culture, and should it do so?

I hope that the experiences of the organisations featured here answer these questions and also serve as role models for others to follow.

WHAT IS ORGANISATIONAL CULTURE?

We all know what culture is, but most of us would find it hard to define. It is a rather vague and slippery idea, but just because a precise definition is hard to frame, that does not mean culture does not exist. It is broadly the pattern of different behaviours that, taken together, comprise 'the way we do things around here'. This way of doing things guides the thinking, behaviour and decision-making of all employees.

Organisational culture can be complex and can vary in different parts of a large organisation. As Edgar H. Schein, an acknowledged expert in corporate culture, points out, 'Wherever a group has enough common experience, a culture begins to form.'[1] Culture can reside at all levels in any system: a country has its own culture, as does a whole industry. There may be an organisational culture but, undoubtedly, there will also be a distinct culture for each department, group or team. Culture can also change over time. As culture affects the way people do things and make decisions, sometimes the changes need to be helped along to ensure the organisation has the right culture in the right place. According to Schein, 'There is now abundant evidence that corporate culture makes a difference to corporate performance.' This is a compelling argument for analysing culture and, where appropriate, seeking to manage its development in a particular direction.

WHAT IS A COACHING CULTURE?

From the organisations I have analysed, it is possible to identify seven clear behaviours that are present to a greater or lesser degree in organisations whose culture is discernibly, though not necessarily exclusively, a coaching culture. It is not clear that any of the organisations studied for this book have yet embedded all these behaviours strongly, but they are well on their way to doing so.

1   Everyone in the organisation believes that learning is critical to individual and organisational success.

2   The leaders of the organisation use a non-directive leadership style, that is, they employ a coaching style with peers and subordinates. This sets the tone for 'the way we do things around here'.

3   Decision-making is devolved as far as possible to those who are closest to having to implement the decisions. They are given freedom to take risks and set their own goals.

4   Managers use a coaching style in the way they manage staff on a day-to-day basis.

5   Managers view developing others and creating a learning environment as being one of their major responsibilities.

6   Peers coach one another to share knowledge, to pass on expertise and to help one another, and also raise their own standards and general standards of professionalism.

7   Having a mentor or a coach is viewed positively, and people are encouraged to seek mentoring or coaching support at various stages in their career and for various reasons (ie when they first join the organisation, on promotion to help someone develop into one or other of their new responsibilities, for the purposes of career development, etc).

WHAT MOTIVATES A BUSINESS TO DEVELOP A COACHING CULTURE?

As Schein points out, organisational culture change will only be successful if the new culture enables the firm to meet its business challenges better. In today's business environment, these challenges are:

- *The need for new ways of leading and managing people.* In recent years, we have witnessed a transformation in people's expectations. People now expect leadership at work, not just management or being told what to do.

- *Knowledge management* is recognised as critical to attaining competitive advantage. The technology that enables knowledge management is increasingly sophisticated and effective but can only be as good as the people who use it.

- Many professional service firms have responded to fierce competitive pressure in the marketplace by *transforming their relationships with clients*. They have moved away from giving their clients solutions and instructions and towards working more in partnership with them to identify issues, explore a range of solutions and problem-solve as a joint enterprise. It is this that has been one of the most powerful drivers for KPMG, whose coaching culture, though still evolving, is well embedded. Its experience is detailed in full at the end of this chapter.

A key driver for the move to a coaching culture at Ernst & Young, according to Mike Laws, Learning and Development Manager, has been the need for knowledge management. Ernst & Young is proud of its knowledge management processes and is an acknowledged leader in the use of such processes. Coaching developed in this organisation as the best way to develop knowledge management.

Competitive pressure has also been a key driver at Ernst & Young. Says Laws:

> There is a strong business drive to be trusted advisers to our clients, and part of this is to facilitate changes in how they think and approach issues. This, in turn, propels us towards a coaching style. Our people have recognised that they need to enable the client, get the client to really think, using their own data. This gets them to rethink their style and stance as business professionals. It is the big business driver around style change.

The KPMG and Ernst & Young experiences in this respect are typical of professional services firms of all kinds – accountants, solicitors, advertising agencies, management consultancies, high-tech businesses and so on. It is in these firms that we see some of the clearest examples of a coaching culture.

WHAT ARE THESE NEW LEADERSHIP STYLES?

In this information age, the primary challenge facing leaders of organisations is to encourage the new, better-educated workforce to be committed, self-managing and life-long learners. This 'people-focused' leadership is founded on the belief that in the complex future 'answers are to be found in community', in group-centred organisations where 'everyone can learn continually'.[2] Followers are being transformed into partners, co-leaders, life-long learners and collaborators.

As the demand for this new leadership grows, the command-and-control leaders at the top of the pyramid are being challenged to change. They are expected to become leaders who are facilitators, stewards, coaches, designers and teachers (Senge 1990[3]).

A number of new leadership models are emerging. The most influential of these are the models that speak of 'collaborative leadership', such as in The Kellogg Leadership Studies Project.[4] While consensus on the name of this 'new leadership' has not been reached, there is consensus on its characteristics. In essence, the new models relate to the idea that you need to be an individual contributor and able to fulfil your personal potential, while also being a member of the team. Employees must see themselves as having freedom, responsibility and discretion; they must feel personally connected to the organisation. They should be confident about their abilities and able to identify the impact they have on the system of which they are part.

An organisation that works on the basis of collaborative leadership does not rely on command-and-control styles but uses continuous, high-quality communication and other management processes that encourage openness, honesty and trust, and that allow for employees to be consulted before decisions are taken. The new leadership models give employees considerable freedom and control over how they organise their work and their time, and over the planning of their work.

Where does coaching come into this?

Coaching is the key delivery mechanism for the new leadership models and is likely to be the prominent style in the organisation. Coaching becomes at once one of the 'delivery mechanisms' in this new way of leading people and the most discernible feature of the organisational culture. As discussed above, sometimes it is the need to move to these new leadership styles that drives the evolution of a coaching culture; sometimes a coaching culture evolves from different business drivers (such as Ernst & Young's focus on knowledge-sharing), and the new leadership styles emerge out of this transformation.

Coaching as a leadership style can be applied to almost all the functions of management: day-to-day issues that need attention, persuading individuals to take on added responsibilities, dealing with problems, addressing improvement of an organisation's services, etc. Applying a coaching style when dealing with direct reports, peers and colleagues is a form of dialogue that uses enquiry and knowledge-sharing in day-to-day conversations, in meetings, and in formal and informal situations.

This approach is in contrast with issuing direct instructions or telling someone 'the right way to do this'. It is an approach that leads people to discover for themselves, to assimilate the knowledge and be able to apply it in other situations. A theme of this book is that because of this and the way it leads to better motivation, it is also the most effective way to encourage the innovation, creativity and entrepreneurship needed to keep pace with change and with competition.

A striking illustration of this was a situation I found a few years ago while working on a consultancy assignment with a recording studio. The managing director of this studio was a charismatic and inspiring leader. He was also the classic entrepreneur. He had already achieved considerable success in the music business and was a well-known figure. He had set up the recording studio but was not interested in the day-to-day running of it, preferring to spend his time doing deals. He was concerned and perplexed, however, by the lack of creativity that was coming from his key personnel, all of whom were highly talented individuals.

As part of my assignment, I carried out an employee opinion survey, using one-to-one confidential interviews. These revealed a surprising message. What all these people valued most was to have occasions when they could get together with the MD either on a one-to-one basis or as a team. What was so valuable about these get-togethers was that the MD had a way of drawing them out, of asking them questions, of getting them to come up with ideas and examine them that enabled them to think 'outside the box' and be creative and innovative. When the dialogue with the MD was missing, these talented, 'creative' people were not able to be creative. Although he did not realise it, this MD was intuitively using a coaching style. He was naturally inquisitive and he instinctively knew that he was not the only one with ideas. In fact, he too benefited from these dialogues as, although he was the one steering the coaching dialogue, the process enabled him to improve and develop his thinking and his ideas.

Although this MD was an 'expert' in the music business, his technique with his staff was to ask 'naïve'[5] questions. What the staff valued was when he sat with them after a recording session and reviewed with them how it went. He would ask questions such as 'How did it go?' 'Did we meet the clients' expectations?' 'What new things did you try this time?' 'What effect did that have?' 'Would you do it again?' 'What did you do for the client to add value?' 'What would you do differently next time?' 'What did you learn from this?' 'What ideas can we take from this for our marketing?' 'What ideas can we take to the next client?' 'What techniques should we be working on and developing?' 'How did you work together?' 'How could you improve on this?'

These questions unleashed much new thinking and creative energy.

Sometimes, clients would come to this business with requests to achieve something technically unusual. The MD would analyse this with his staff: 'What is the problem?' 'What is the client aiming for?' 'How experienced is the client?' 'What are the options open to the client?' 'How can we satisfy the client within these constraints?'

When he was not there, none of this happened, and the staff and the business suffered. What he had failed to do in his organisation was pass on his coaching technique to his staff so that they could coach one another. For his business to thrive and grow the way he wanted it to, and in a way that would enable him to take a back seat, he needed to establish a coaching culture.

But for the culture of an organisation to be a coaching culture, it must be recognised that coaching is more than an act of dialogue: it is also about people-oriented management processes.

What are these people-oriented management processes, and how do they work?

The way people are recruited, managed, motivated and rewarded needs to be consistent with the values of the organisation and what it is trying to achieve.

The starting point, therefore, is what the organisation stands for and its principal strategic aims. These are often set out in a vision or mission statement or the principles of the organisation's 'employer brand'.

In a coaching culture, people must share important values and feel they are part of a corporate culture that emphasises the importance of the organisation's human assets. Since the organisation needs people to share knowledge, work in teams and respect confidences, the members must display trust, openness and respect for each other. They must be committed to the idea that sharing knowledge does not diminish them but raises them, together with the organisation. Clearly, such a culture will not take hold in an organisation that is internally highly competitive and aggressive. When people are trying to climb to the top over the bodies of their colleagues – and many such organisations do exist – then it stands to reason that they will resist sharing skills and knowledge for the common good. Rather, they will seek to trade knowledge with their colleagues in return for status.

Many organisations have a vision statement or have developed an employer brand that supports their organisational culture. These set guidelines make clear what the organisation is aiming for, what it stands for and what behaviour is expected from staff.

An example of this is the Ernst & Young vision, which emphasises the importance of putting their people and clients first. It is a virtuous circle of adding value to people who then add value to clients. This type of emphasis promotes openness and teamwork through participation in organisational decision-making. Employees feel that the people in their unit can work together to solve problems and that their ideas are valued and taken seriously.

Out of this emphasis on people comes a growing openness in the firm that it is all right to be coached and that coaching is about doing even better. The message is put across consistently, so that it is clear that it is important to learn, develop, continuously improve and seek help in order to do so. This is now a strong ethos at Ernst & Young.

PwC also believes coaching to be well integrated into its organisational culture. As Moira Siddons describes it:

> Coaching keeps the business moving and it chips away at persistent problems. It changes the culture. It encourages a more open communication process and our people are more prepared to take responsibility for themselves. It is all too easy for people to project their own inadequacies onto others but a coaching culture changes this and gets people to think 'How can I make a difference, be different, help others?' It drives home personal accountability. At PwC, there is a strong belief in personal development, in self-awareness and behavioural impact.

How does the organisation promote the message so that the vision statement or brand identity become more than empty words?

These clearly identified behaviours need to be talked about as much as possible, at formal meetings and informal 'corridor' conversations, so as to constantly raise awareness and get people to carve out their own roles to fit within this overall framework. It is not about being prescriptive. It is about giving clear parameters and guidelines.

The way work is organised is also critical. People value autonomy and control. This is particularly true of 'knowledge workers' but is becoming more the norm in every workplace. The old adage about mushroom management – 'Keep them in the dark and feed them manure' – is no longer a joke. Workers confronted with this approach will vote with their feet and find other jobs or, if they stay, will be poorly motivated and angry. People in the workplace are independent and want to have a voice in matters that affect them, including which projects they work on and which ones they don't. They want to be consulted on wider issues in the workplace and to feel their views are valued. People want to be affiliated to teams to work with like-minded people they can learn from. They want to feel they belong and that people care about them.

Formal and informal communication at all levels and across the organisation is essential. Informal links become more difficult to establish the larger the organisation, and there needs to be a good mix of occasions so that people can come together informally, such as through special lunches, refreshments and social gatherings. Formal communication systems are equally vital: there needs to be a wide range of these (at presentations, regular and *ad hoc* meetings, etc); and they need to include regular department meetings and team meetings. An important element of the mix is listening. Employee opinion surveys, focus groups and other occasions for listening to what employees have to say and harnessing their ideas are invaluable. KPMG, Ernst & Young and PwC, for example, survey their employees frequently, and for many different reasons.

What other HR processes suit a coaching culture?

There are a number of other people-management processes that are found in organisations with coaching cultures, or that are appropriate to underpin such a culture. The following are the main ones.

Succession planning

Coaching has an important role in succession planning. Firm growth, leadership turnover and career life cycles have a compounding effect on the supply and demand of leaders. The challenges of filling leadership positions from the outside cause most firms to grow leadership talent from within. In their research into professional service firms, published in their book *Aligning the Stars*, Lorsch and Tiernay[5] found that 'successful, enduring [professional service] firms understand the risk, as do their chief executives. These chief executives continually analyse their leadership supply and demand, planning at least five years in advance.' Lorsch and Tiernay established that these firms invest heavily in leadership development, with on-the-job learning and personal mentoring being the most effective tactics.

Appraisal and feedback

Coaching is highly effective when used to give people feedback on their performance. This is true both of 'real-time' feedback (ie giving people immediate feedback on a piece of work and how they handled it) and also longer-term feedback such as through the performance review process. Mike Laws at Ernst & Young finds a strong correlation between using a coaching style to give feedback on performance and work satisfaction: 'Coaching is as important as all other learning and people processes. It involves giving "quality time", concentrating on an individual and their needs, as well as demonstrating an interest in people. People respond well to the attention but also to the setting of targets and the effort to improve performance.' Lorsch and Tierney also stress the value of real-time feedback in developing and managing people (see Chapter 2).

Personal development and career planning

Processes that focus on personal development and career planning for all staff are a vital part of a coaching culture. Such a plan may include: feedback on performance as a regular activity, not a once-a-year ritual; the allocation of a personal coach at different times and for different reasons; opportunities to take part in special projects or assignments or to work on different teams; and high-quality training and development opportunities.

A study carried out by Egon Zehnder in Atlanta has found that organisations are increasingly measuring their top executives on how they evaluate, coach and develop professionals in their group.[6]

360-degree feedback

360-degree feedback on performance is a highly effective development tool that is being used by many organisations to help people shift their behaviour and develop key skills. It also works well with a coaching approach.

A senior vice-president of the New York office of one of the US's largest banks describes the process in his bank:

> *The culture of the organisation has been shifting for the past two years towards what you are describing as a 'coaching culture'. We have quarterly 360°-reviews by our peers and colleagues that are carried out online. The data is shared confidentially with the individual. People are being given the chance to keep the data private but they are expected to use it for developing the key, people-oriented behaviours that the organisation has identified as being critical to success. It is likely that this will change soon and the individual will have to share their 360°-data with their line manager and it will be used for review purposes. At such time, there is likely to be a fall-out from those people who cannot adapt, or who just do not wish to. Some voluntary fall-out has already been happening.*

Talent management programmes

The Egon Zehnder study, referred to above, also reveals that increasing numbers of companies are introducing 'talent management' programmes, aimed at treating the top 20 per cent of performers who drive and deliver superior results in an exceptional and individualised way, especially as regards evaluation, reward and retention.

Bruce Tulgan, a US management consultant and author of *Winning the Talent Wars*,[7] was a speaker at the CIPD's (Chartered Institute of Personnel and Development) Annual Recruitment Conference, 2001, in London. He set out the following ways of managing talent:

- segment different performance levels
- focus on the retention rate of best and low performers, rather than on overall attrition and retention rates
- retain your best performers as long as possible
- invest in social capital – people are loyal to teams, so make the group strong.

The American bank mentioned above operates along these lines. The senior vice-president comments that the bank divides its talent pool into the top 20 per cent of performers and the bottom 10 per cent. Efforts are made to develop the bottom 10 per cent and help them improve their performance, but inevitably a number are 'let go'. The senior vice-president predicts that the organisation will become known as a first-rate training ground. Those whose stay there is short will nonetheless be highly sought after in the job market.

I have previously worked for an American multinational that operated a policy of this nature to good effect. However, it requires careful management. It can easily lead to an aggressive, combative work environment where knowledge is not shared and where people neither seek help nor seek to learn for fear of showing weakness. Clearly, this is not what a coaching culture aims to achieve.

Learning and development

We have already mentioned that organisations with a strong coaching culture have an ethos that positively encourages people to learn, develop, seek feedback and seek help. Buddies, internal coaches and mentors and external coaches are widely available to staff for a range of reasons. These reasons might include: to help new recruits understand the organisation and find their way around; for graduate and other trainees, to help their career development; for people newly appointed to a role, to help them learn and develop their new skills, and so on.

Also widely available are training and other learning programmes including courses to help people develop their coaching skills. At Ernst & Young and PwC, for example, coaching is open to all staff. Ernst & Young estimate that around 80 per cent of its staff have access to coaching. Both organisations generally use internal coaches for staff below partner level. When arranging coaching for partners, however, it is sometimes felt preferable to appoint external coaches who are not influenced by internal politics, bring in fresh views and understanding, and with whom the partners may feel more open.

Learning increases a person's market value and mostly occurs on the job. While the organisation may not want to invest in practical and marketable education that will assist staff to move elsewhere, it is necessary to provide just that in order to attract the best applicants, to enable them to perform their current roles effectively and to develop them for future roles. It is then up to the organisation to retain them by the use of other mechanisms, particularly the work they are given, which needs to be constantly challenging and developing. People also want career options: they seldom think of their current job or organisation as an end point; it is simply one phase in a career. High-fliers, in particular, will evaluate whether your organisation will open future doors for them and whether it will continue to help them develop and make them more marketable in the years ahead. To retain them the organisation must offer both career prospects and development opportunities.

What reward systems are needed in a coaching culture?

Lorsch and Tierney[8] emphasise the importance of reflecting people-oriented values in the reward systems. They cite Bain & Co, where one of the five criteria used to determine compensation is 'people asset building', which includes mentoring, coaching and developing others within the case-team setting and outside it. They also use as an example Goldman Sachs, where mentoring, coaching and recruiting are on the list of qualitative criteria used to evaluate part-ner (now director) performance.

The organisations I have featured in this chapter have not formally incorporated their people-oriented values in their reward systems, though they all believe that these values are suffi-ciently well-embedded for people to see them as the way to achieve increased fees, profits and other financial and business targets. Perhaps, in years to come, we will see a move towards direct reward of success against people management criteria.

Ernst & Young introduced the balanced scorecard approach in about 2000, and this incorpo-rates people-oriented targets. The balanced scorecard was developed by Robert S. Kaplan and David P. Norton in 1992[9] and is reportedly used by 60 per cent of the Fortune 1000 companies.[10] It provides managers with a presentation of both financial and operational measures that give them a fast but comprehensive view of the business. The system includes financial measures that summarise the results of actions already taken. These are complemented with operational measures on customer satisfaction, internal processes and innovation, and learning and growth. An example of a learning and growth measure might be, 'Everyone completes a self-evaluation and all managers carry out performance appraisals of the people who work with them'.

What control systems are used in organisations that have a coaching culture?

Discipline and control must be clearly defined in all organisations, but this is especially so in a coaching culture. In a coaching culture, people report that their organisations provide clear goals, clear lines of authority and clear task responsibilities. While they have autonomy, they are aware of the boundaries of their decision-making discretion. They know what they are responsible for and what others have responsibility for achieving. In financial services companies many people have financial limits within which they can make decisions without needing to refer to a higher authority. Without this basic level of structure and control, employees experience chaos rather than empowerment.

A coaching culture also provides people with support and a sense of security. In order to feel that the system really wants empowered employees, individuals need a sense of social support from their bosses, peers and subordinates. Employees' efforts to take initiative and risk must be reinforced rather than punished. If this support is missing or weak, employees will worry about seeking permission before acting, rather than asking for forgiveness in case they make mistakes. They must believe that the company will support them as they learn and grow.

Many people value flexibility, and flexible working systems are rapidly becoming a characteris-tic of the coaching culture. In such organisations, hours of work are not specified in contracts of employment, which instead specify the goals and outcomes that people need to achieve and in what time period.

How does an organisation achieve a coaching culture?

Before being able to address this question of how an organisation can achieve a coaching culture, it is useful to look at how you can change organisational culture.

How do you change organisational culture?

Schein[11] describes culture change in a mature organisation as first and foremost about unlearning and predictable resistance to change. To encourage people to learn new behaviours and overcome resistance, a planned, managed change process is necessary. A steering committee, or an equivalent, must be responsible for conceptualising the new way of thinking and behaving. The old culture needs to be assessed in terms of where it aids or hinders the needed changes in business processes.

Schein warns that a culture change is likely to be painful and may take some years to accomplish and involve many casualties on the way. He also warns that you may not know if your new culture is successful for some time. He emphasises that 'only with repeated success do the new ways of thinking and working become a new culture in its own right'.

Schein's observations are borne out by the experiences of the organisations featured in this chapter. In all cases, a coaching culture has been evolving over many years. It has been influenced strongly by an individual, or a group of individuals. Although there is no definition of a coaching culture in these organisations, the values, mission, goals and management processes have all been designed to promote and reinforce messages that are consistent with a coaching culture. The effectiveness of a 'coaching way of doing things' is discernible, and this creates its own momentum.

At Ernst & Young, for example, the transition to a coaching culture commenced in the mid-1990s. It was started in the company's south region, and efforts are being made to encourage its spread to other parts of the organisation. The HR function first used coaching as a way of learning and knowledge-sharing within its own team and then with its 'clients' within the organisation. From there developed the notion that a coaching style would benefit employees for use with their clients and for purposes of knowledge-sharing. The HR team identified 12 people to be 'champion coaches'. These 12 were selected for their predisposition towards coaching and not because of their role or seniority.

The managing partner was highly supportive, and he too became a 'champion coach'. The champion coaches started using coaching with their clients and colleagues. The benefits became talked about and led to a growing awareness that this was a style that improved personal relationships within the firm and with clients. It took some time to persuade employees to work in this different way with clients and to encourage them to 'let go' of the notion that they had to have a complete answer or action plan to present to the client. To develop a coaching culture, it is necessary to take small steps and achieve small shifts in awareness.

The key question, however, is whether this is an indulgence or whether it leads to increased profitability. The organisations featured in this chapter survey their staff regularly, and these surveys indicate that a coaching culture indeed leads to increased levels of work satisfaction and motivation, and that this in turn aids retention. Certainly, the organisations featured here are all generally held to be among the best employers, based on various measures such as *The Sunday Times* annual 'best company' survey.

What are the obstacles to being able to develop a coaching culture?

A coaching culture is a different way of doing things and, like all techniques and behaviour, is rooted in attitudes and values. The biggest obstacle is therefore getting people to 'buy in', to take the idea on board so that they change their attitudes and with that their behaviour. There are some personalities who do not readily warm to a coaching culture. It is also difficult, at the best of times, to influence the behaviours people adopt at work. There is a long history of trying to establish learning organisations and initiate culture change programmes by directing these from the top, or from the HR department. To add to this, being directive, telling people 'what to do', goes completely against the spirit of a coaching culture and so is an especially inadvisable approach to attempt. Rather, a coaching culture and coaching initiatives need to be enabled, in much the same way as we have seen at Ernst & Young and as is set out in the KPMG case study. This can be a slow process.

A significant obstacle to the coaching culture lies in the British psyche as, perhaps, in several other European nations. As a national culture, the British shy away from expressing feelings and revealing too much of themselves, especially avoiding admission of any weakness. In the US, where coaching is more embedded, there exists a strong self-help culture. Many Americans are more than happy to talk about themselves; they are familiar with using therapists for personal problems.

The approach to implementing a coaching culture must take account of such cultural differences. In spite of natural British reticence, the use of coaching in all its guises is increasing in the UK, as people realise the benefits of one-to-one, confidential support. But it does mean that it needs to become a well-established feeling and philosophy that it is acceptable to seek help. It is also important for the message to clearly portray coaching as developmental and not remedial, as part of the learning process and as a way of enabling people to fulfil their personal development needs. Coaching also needs to be strongly associated with success.

I see a 'coaching culture' as the successor to the concept of the learning organisation. The learning organisation is a theory of organisations as 'learning systems' in which success depends on two key skills: learning continuously and giving direction. I believe the learning organisation debate has succeeded but to a limited degree only: it has helped change attitudes and got people individually to recognise the importance of learning. It has helped people see learning as something they themselves need to take control of, as opposed to its being something that is 'done' to them by being sent on a training course.

I do not believe, however, that it has had much impact on the way people and relationships are managed in the organisation. Perhaps this is because the learning organisation theory lacked a sharp business focus. In contrast, the concept of a 'coaching culture' does have that sharp business focus. As we have seen in this chapter, and as is clearly illustrated in the following case study, the instigation of a coaching culture is driven by strong business imperatives. It is because of this that the coaching organisation will become recognised as the shape and nature of the organisation of today.

CASE STUDY

A coaching culture at KPMG

Background

In this case study, we look at how KPMG, one of the world's leading professional services firms, employing approximately 9,500 people in the UK, is successfully developing a coaching culture. We also relate KPMG's experience with the points raised in this chapter.

Coaching has always been an integral element of the culture of KPMG – it is the way people work with one another and their clients. In recent years, coaching has become embedded into the partner admissions process, and the firm now has a number of people at a senior level who have experienced coaching and fully appreciate its importance to individuals and hence the firm. One-to-one coaching is increasingly sought out by individuals on all aspects of personal development and career management.

What are the business imperatives for a coaching culture?

Coaching is one of KPMG's strategic levers for change. The firm recognises that a coaching culture is key in any organisation that relishes change and understands the value that embracing it intelligently can give. Learning to live with change places a premium on one competency above all others: learning to learn (and to unlearn).

How does coaching mesh with organisational processes?

KPMG has three global values – clients, people and knowledge – and these underpin the firm's performance management process. Coaching in all its forms helps to ensure that these values are embedded into the organisation by creating an environment where knowledge is shared, people learn and the firm is more able to meet the needs of its clients, providing them with the standard of service they both need and expect.

KPMG has a number of internal processes and development activities that may give rise to a specific coaching need. These include 360-degree feedback, performance management discussions and the firm's senior manager and partner development and assessment process. Coaching is not automatically provided to individuals – the emphasis is on ensuring that everyone associated with the processes and activities is aware of how coaching might be used and knows how to access it.

What does a coaching culture mean in KPMG?

Within KPMG, a coaching culture refers to the quality of helpfulness that exists within the firm. This can be categorised under two main headings:

People's mindset in terms of the way they operate and relate to one another, for example:
- when developing an idea, doing so with a coaching and enabling leadership style
- encouraging and enabling coaching and mentoring processes
- encouraging and supporting an environment where people feel motivated and encouraged and receive timely and constructive feedback
- continuing to enhance the quality of performance management processes.

The accessibility and availability of more structured help, for example:

- the accessibility of coaching following specific development activities
- having learning and knowledge management tools that provide intelligent information and that help people to make the right decisions.

How does KPMG define coaching?

Coaching encompasses a broad range of activities within the firm, which has produced definitions to help people think about their role as a coach and the knowledge and skills they are looking for when they seek coaching from others.

Sharing experiences/learning to help someone to be more effective in their role/life includes:

- on-the-job mentoring
- using a colleague as a sounding board on a client or risk management issue
- the mentoring of new partners by more senior partners.

Helping someone to develop their own approach to an issue includes:

- skill development coaching to capitalise on an existing strength or address a development need – such as after a senior manager development centre or partner assessment centre
- developing a strategy for a significant new role, including where there may be little or no precedent for it
- helping someone to take a long-term view of managing their career.

The provision of expert skills to problems that can be regarded as more deep-seated. This might include situations where someone needs to:

- recover confidence
- develop coping strategies for stressful situations.

The manager as coach

Coaching is an integral part of a manager's role and includes:

- encouraging, motivating and developing others
- helping people to access development opportunities and more structured coaching and mentoring where it is needed.

What coaching resources are available to support a coaching culture?

The firm has an extensive range of resources available to individuals to support and drive a coaching culture. These can be categorised under three headings:

People

The people available include:

- internal consultants, comprising: career coaches, learning and development coaches and internal HR consultants.
- external consultants. The firm has a faculty of external coaches who are able to bring specific skills experience to some coaching situations, particularly those arising during the partner admissions process.

Information

The firm provides web-based guidance to help staff access the resources they need. This includes guidance on:

- developing coaching skills
- identifying a coach to meet a specific need
- coaching support available following specific development and assessment processes and activities
- the range of local coaching activities taking place within the firm.

Activities

These include:

- formal coaching skills development programmes and local drop-in clinics to meet needs on a just-in-time basis
- regular opportunities for people in formal internal coaching roles to share their learning and experiences in supporting and driving a coaching culture.

How do people justify taking time out to coach?

Coaching is regarded as an integral part of the role of everyone in KPMG. The firm believes that everyone has a right to expect coaching from others within the firm – and a responsibility to provide it. While financial measures of performance are sometimes seen as a deterrent to investing time in coaching, feedback indicates that the firm provides an environment that encourages and supports coaching, in all its forms.

How are the results of coaching measured?

The effectiveness of coaching is measured in terms of behavioural change. Internal surveys are the key source of evidence of broader cultural change.

(This case study was jointly written with John Bailey, Director of Coaching, KPMG)

KEY LEARNING POINTS ON COACHING AS AN ORGANISATIONAL CULTURE

It is difficult, but not impossible, to change the culture of the organisation. Real change to an organisation's culture involves winning the hearts and minds of the people within it. The business reasons for change must be clear.

A coaching culture places emphasis on learning, development and knowledge-sharing. It is about leading people using a collaborative, non-directive style. It is ideally suited to today's business environment.

A coaching culture is reinforced and underpinned by leadership styles and management processes that encourage the desired values and behaviours.

A coaching organisation takes every opportunity to promote the concept of coaching. Coaching, provided either by internal or external coaches, is widely available to most staff and is seen as developmental and beneficial. Resources to inform people about coaching, support the development of coaching skills and encourage conversations about coaching are available.

A coaching culture is not prescriptive. It emphasises desired behaviours and encourages people to adopt these but does not enforce them.

A coaching culture needs to evolve, but this evolution can be started and helped along through vision and by identifying people to champion the culture by role-modelling the behaviours. When coaching achieves visible success, this spearheads its evolution and its adoption throughout the organisation.

A coaching culture is a way of doing things that is exceptionally well-suited to today's business environment. It does not necessarily involve a change of orientation from being focused on results, profits and competitiveness. Rather, it requires recognition that people-oriented leadership affects these goals positively.

NOTES AND REFERENCES

1 SCHEIN E. H. (1999) *The Corporate Culture Survival Guide.* San Francisco, Jossey-Bass.

2 LORSCH J. W. *and* TIERNEY T. J. (2002) *Aligning the Stars.* Massachusetts, Harvard Business School Press.

3 SENGE P. (1990) *The Art of and Practice of the Learning Organisation.* New York, Doubleday.

4 KELLERMAN B. (1998) 'The Kellogg Leadership Studies Project: Rethinking Leadership Working Papers' *The Kellogg Leadership Studies Project.* Maryland USA, Academy of Leadership Press.

5 LORSCH J. W. *and* TIERNEY T. J. (2002) *Aligning the Stars.* Massachusetts, Harvard Business School Press.

6 DIETZ A. (2003) *Talent Management Boom Could be Good for You.* Atlanta, Eagon Zehnder International. see www.careerjournal.com.

7   TULGAN B. (2001) *Winning the Talent Wars and Managing Generation X.* New York, Norton WW & Company.

8   LORSCH J. W. *and* TIERNEY T. J. (2002) *Aligning the Stars.* Massachusetts, Harvard Business School Press.

9   KAPLAN R. S *and* NORTON D. P. (1992) 'Putting the balanced scorecard to work'. *Harvard Business Review.* January – February.

10 PONSARD J. *and* SAULPIC O. (1998) Cahier no. 2002–010, Ecole Poytechnique Scientifique.

11 SCHEIN E. H. (1999) *The Corporate Culture Survival Guide.* San Francisco, Jossey-Bass.

2

Coaching as a management style

A coaching style of management is one where the manager uses coaching techniques in discussions and dealings with staff. By using these techniques, the manager encourages the employee to identify options and seek his or her own solutions to problems. This style is in direct contrast to a directive one where the manager has the answer and tells the employee how it should be done. It is a style of management that is more appropriate and more productive in today's organisations because of changing attitudes to authority. In addition a manager may also work with an employee on a more formal coaching basis, perhaps to help that person develop their knowledge or acquire a new skill or responsibility.

This chapter explores such issues as: What is a coaching style of management? When should a coaching style be used? What are the main techniques and models? How should you coach high and poor performers? What if someone does not respond to being coached by their manager? How can an organisation encourage managers to adopt a coaching style? Can a coaching style be effective in a command-and-control culture? How can we develop managers to be coaches?

WHAT IS A COACHING STYLE OF MANAGEMENT?

A coaching style of management is not about 'being the boss', giving directions and instructions and telling people what to do, or how they should have done it, or jumping in with the answer. Rather, a leader's role today is to enable, encourage and facilitate so that staff have a stronger sense of control over their own work and their own time, and so that they identify their own options and solutions to problems. To achieve this the manager also needs to act as a role model of the desired behaviours. Nonetheless, there may be times when the manager will still need to be more directive with a member of staff.

A coaching style of management therefore embraces the following range of styles:

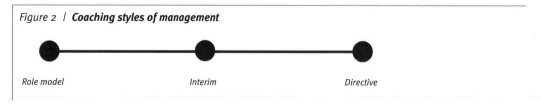

Figure 2 | *Coaching styles of management*

Role model   Interim   Directive

At the first stage on the continuum, a manager needs to role-model the behaviours that are critical to successful performance and that reinforce the values of your team and the organisation. You need to have a clear vision and put this across consistently. If you do this effectively, standards of performance will be clear; others will easily identify them and put them into effect.

Use interim styles where your intervention is required. For instance, where you are actively coaching someone to identify their own need and work out the solution that suits them best but they are unable to do this, then you need to move into a more directive style. It is likely, with an inexperienced team member, that you will need to use a directive style more frequently. To enable you to decide which of these styles to use and when, you need to weigh up how willing, committed and experienced the team member is and how complex the task is in relation to their level of experience.

'It's a SNIP'[1]

Whether you are coaching in spontaneous circumstances or more formally, it is essential to follow a process. This is essential to ensuring the discussion remains focused and achieves the desired result.

The following model may be helpful to you:

S situation
Ask the learner to describe the situation you wish to discuss. They should set out the problem or issue, giving specific examples and background information.

N need
Ask the learner to identify the need. What do they need to do differently? Or what needs to change or be learned? This will enable them to describe the desired outcome. As they do this some options may start to emerge, or barriers may be identified. Don't try to solve these but note them and any emerging ideas.

I ideas
Stimulate the learner to identify ideas that they would feel comfortable with and that would meet their need. One technique for encouraging the flow of ideas is to identify any barriers that are preventing the learner from using the desired behaviours. Sort these into:

- employee blocks such as lack of skills or knowledge, or low motivation
- blocks that exist in others, such as anxious customers, stressed colleagues or a panicky manager
- blocks that exist in situations, such as inadequate resources or unexpected shifting in deadlines.

Jointly brainstorm ways around these blocks and identify the possible next steps or solutions.

P plan
Ideally, the person will by now have identified an appropriate solution and you can agree a plan to include actions and timing.

If the person is unable to find a solution, it is probably appropriate then to be more directive and give advice.

It may also be appropriate to follow through with your learner at a later stage, to find out how they got on with the problem and what happened, and to see if any further coaching is required.

The following situation, described by a banker in New York, illustrates this model:

> One of our major clients approached us about a transaction. We gave them good advice, but they did not take it and instead gave the business to another bank, which had said they would do the deal on their terms. In the event, this rival bank was unable to deliver and so the client asked us to come into the deal, by this time desperate for our help in bailing them out of a difficult situation.

> The executive on my team who was dealing with this client was all for immediately accepting the client's offer. I had a different view. I believed that the client had treated us badly and that if we shrugged this off we might find ourselves in a similar position with them in the future, where they would shop around first and only use us as a last resort. I wanted a discussion with the client about our long-term relationship with them. I wanted, if not a commitment, at least an indication that they would continue using us as their advisers, once this transaction was complete. I felt it was better for all of us to have a frank discussion, clear the air and talk about what would happen next.

> If I had just put my point of view to my executive (who was willing and committed but not that well experienced), the likelihood was that he would accept it grudgingly and this would not help either how he handled the situation or how he might handle other client relationships. I used a coaching style with him, along these lines: 'What is your view of our position in respect of this deal?' was my initial (situation) question, getting him first of all to acknowledge and think through how we had been treated. 'How does the client view our position?' (need) Here I was hoping that he would acknowledge that the client needs to recognise they have put us in a difficult position, and why.

> There was a junior executive present during this conversation. She immediately saw where the questions were leading and jumped in: 'Are we sure we are dealing with the decision-maker?' 'Do we have the right access?' 'Does the CEO appreciate how we feel?' (ideas) By this time, the executive started to work out what he was going to do next and how he would handle the situation (plan). If he had not, I would have switched to telling mode. By avoiding the directive style in the way I did, I, in fact, achieved a better result, as the junior executive had identified some other problems of which I was unaware.

The same US banker describes the following situation:

> I went to a client meeting with two of my staff and I came out feeling that we had not been sufficiently well prepared. I did not want to just come straight out and say so. I believe that is ineffective. I also did not want to tell them how it should be done. Instead, I suggested we should all get together to talk about how we handle client meetings in general. At our get-together, I asked the following questions: 'What did you feel about the meeting?' (situation) 'What went well?' 'We had such-and-such a problem – how did that arise?' (need) 'What should we have done? (ideas)

By the end of the discussion, we had a blueprint (plan) for handling meetings, and my two colleagues always prepare well now and have considerably improved their ratio of 'sales meetings to winning the deal'. I also analysed my own position. I now make a point of making sure I role-model the desired behaviour and always prepare adequately for a meeting, and I also make sure that 'preparation' is something we talk about when discussing future client meetings.

WHEN SHOULD A COACHING STYLE BE USED?

There are many reasons for coaching. These can broadly be grouped into two: coaching in spontaneous circumstances, and coaching to enhance learning and development.

The aim should be for coaching to be part of how managers and staff do things on a normal, day-to-day basis. With coaching you have an opportunity to improve the way you manage, develop your staff, plan for succession, and share knowledge and expertise. You may need to help someone inexperienced to develop a new skill or take on a new responsibility. You may need to coach a poor performer to help that person reach the desired standard. You may need to find time to help someone sort out a problem, or to assist someone broaden their skills and knowledge to prepare them for promotion.

Spontaneous coaching

In many cases, it is not necessary to set aside times for special meetings labelled 'coaching'. There is more to be gained from changing the style of discussions and taking advantage of naturally occurring coaching opportunities, such as when a member of staff comes in to ask something, or during a review meeting, while walking down the corridor, or travelling together. I call this kind of coaching 'spontaneous coaching', but it is sometimes called 'seize-the-moment coaching' or 'laser coaching'.

As, by definition, you are unlikely to have much time to prepare for coaching in spontaneous circumstances, I recommend any manager to become thoroughly familiar with the 'SNIP' model described above. It will then be second nature to apply an appropriate structure to the discussion.

FORMAL COACHING FOR LEARNING AND DEVELOPMENT

It is now recognised that a great deal of learning takes place on the job.

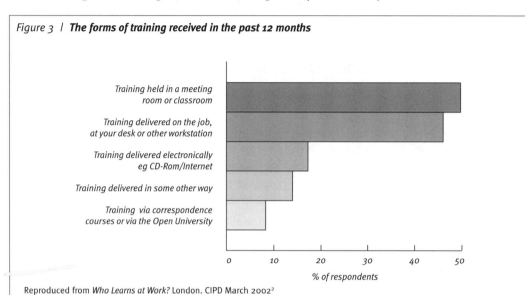

Figure 3 | **The forms of training received in the past 12 months**

Reproduced from *Who Learns at Work?* London. CIPD March 2002[2]

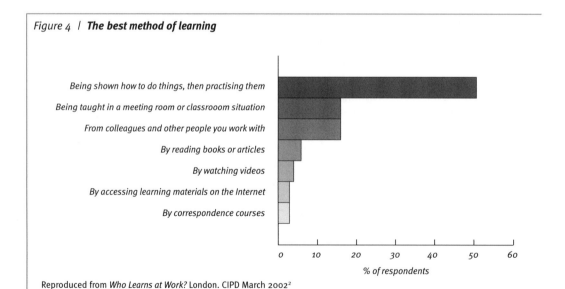

Figure 4 | **The best method of learning**

Reproduced from *Who Learns at Work?* London. CIPD March 2002[2]

Coaching is an effective way of learning on the job because it is informal and incidental. It is an opportunity to learn at the very point at which the need for a new skill or piece of knowledge becomes apparent. Immediate coaching ensures that practice reinforces the learning. Ideally, coaching is non-threatening because it focuses on behaviour rather than results and because the coach manages the process in such a way that employees have the experience of developing skills for themselves rather than simply being 'told what to do'.

On-the-job learning does not just happen, however. Certain conditions are important:

1   The learner needs to reflect on the learning.

2   The learner needs real-time feedback.

3   The learner needs to be given work that furthers his or her development.

1 ENHANCING LEARNING THROUGH REFLECTION

Reflective learning is especially important for translating on-the-job experience into on-the-job learning.

The thinking behind reflective learning is that learning does not just happen on its own. For people to learn from their work, they need to be conscious they are doing so.

The following reflective learning cycle[3] shows the different stages of learning.

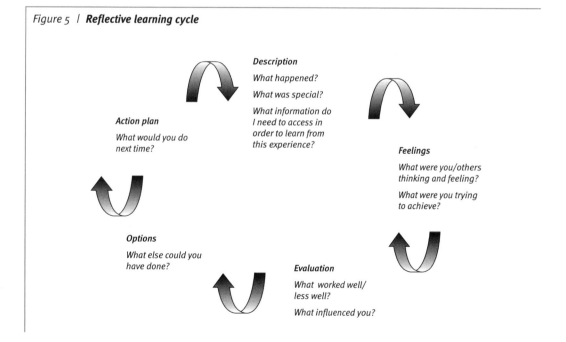

Figure 5 | *Reflective learning cycle*

Description
What happened?
What was special?
What information do I need to access in order to learn from this experience?

Action plan
What would you do next time?

Feelings
What were you/others thinking and feeling?
What were you trying to achieve?

Options
What else could you have done?

Evaluation
What worked well/ less well?
What influenced you?

The question at the heart of the cycle is: 'What information do I need to access in order to learn from this experience?' As you go through the cycle, you need to keep asking questions:

- *Description of the experience*: What happened? What was special about the experience?

- *Feelings (reflection)*: What was I trying to achieve? Why did I intervene as I did? What were the consequences? What did I feel? What did others feel?

- *Evaluation*: What worked well? What did not work well? What internal and external factors influenced my decision-making, and what sources of knowledge did or should have influenced me? Could I have dealt better with the situation? What other choices were there and what might have been their consequences?

    How do I now feel about this experience, and how have I made sense of it in the light of past experiences and future practice? How has this experience changed my ways of knowing: the empirics, the aesthetics, the ethics, personal aspects?

- *Options*: What else could I have done? Were my actions the optimum of the possibilities open to me?

- *Action plan*: What will I do next time?

Managers have a role in encouraging individuals to learn reflectively as regularly as possible. It can also be especially valuable to use this cycle to learn together as a team.

2 ENHANCING LEARNING THROUGH REAL-TIME FEEDBACK

Informal, immediate feedback helps someone learn. It is also tremendously motivating when a more senior person in an organisation takes the trouble to think about them, or takes the time to explain a decision, or challenges them to think beyond their specific task. They are not only strengthening the employee's technical skills but also demonstrating the organisation's concern for their development. When the feedback comes from a fellow team member, it increases a sense of belonging. Feedback is an especially good way of strengthening and developing relationships.

This is a comment made by a sales director to one of her associates when they were travelling back from a client meeting:

> *Your response to the client's objection was well-handled. I was impressed with the way you kept calm and kept asking questions to get to the bottom of what they were thinking. Next time, once the client agrees to the point, just move on and then refer again to their agreement when summing up the action points. You laboured the point a bit too much, I feel, by getting them to keep repeating their agreement.*

It is important to give people specific, positive feedback that helps them identify what they did well and what they should do more of. Equally, feedback that identifies areas for improvement helps people develop and, when it is delivered in a direct and constructive way, strengthens relationships.

3 ENHANCING SKILLS THROUGH WORK

Interesting and challenging work as well as opportunities to develop new skills and knowledge are recognised as being key motivators for many people. Receiving coaching from a more senior manager is a key tool that encourages greater delegation of work and therefore encourages employees to take greater ownership of work. This, in turn, reduces the manager's workload and creates more development possibilities for both the manager and his or her team members.

One line manager in the operations department of a London bank has assigned to her, every year, two or three of the bank's graduate trainees who are on a 'tour' around the different areas of the bank. She describes how her coaching style helps both them and her:

> *I am currently responsible for three graduate trainees. I have to teach them product knowledge, how to solve problems, how to approach people and operate in a large organisation and also help them develop their technical knowledge.*

> *On one occasion, I had to do a sales presentation and I decided to delegate the preparation of this to one of the trainees. Before going on a coaching skills training course, I was very directive in my approach to the graduate trainees. Previously, I would have said 'Do it this way', 'Put in that'. I would have had all the answers. Now, I use a coaching style; as a result, the graduate designed a sophisticated, interactive slide show. The content was essentially dry but he presented it intuitively so that it was fun and human. He achieved this because he was forced to do more of the thinking himself. We all benefited. I had a better end result and he had learned much more.*

> *One of the graduates who was with me last year has spoken of how positive the experience has been in my team and has said he feels he has done so well. He has really bought into the coaching approaches I use with him and has internalised them so that he is already passing them on to those he works with now and is well on his way to being given staff responsibility.*

Coaching high and poor performers

Managers need to be able to coach poor and high performers. With high performers the manager must provide plenty of real-time feedback while ensuring the individual is given maximum exposure to new, interesting and challenging work. Referring to the coaching styles continuum, the manager will be at the left-hand side, using role-model and interim coaching styles.

With poor performers it is likely that the manager will need to be more directive.

A manager with a British-based organisation describes the approach she has been taking with someone in an overseas branch who was not performing to the standards required.

> *Our sales team in Madrid has a team leader who is off sick and likely to be away for some time. I am managing the team, from London, in her absence. The more senior of the staff in the office has some 'inappropriate' behaviours and I am working on these with him. Until six weeks ago, he had not written a single report or participated in our deal review process. He is basically a maverick. He has just been doing his own thing and not following procedures or documenting anything. I am getting him to write things down now, or at least tell me about them so I can document them. We have now written six or seven accounting plans. Previously, they were in his head. We have weekly meetings on the telephone and I go there regularly.*

I am driving hard to get the business in but want him to initiate the process and the communication flow. I think he felt isolated before. I listen to him. I go through things slowly and steadily and talk about a transaction with him and together we talk about how to approach it and how to handle the client. I encourage him to participate by using the coaching process (as in the SNIP model above) *and getting him to identify the problem, but I always end up having to be directive and give the answer. At least, I get him to work it through. That way he finds my answer more acceptable and he is more likely to follow it than if I just told him what to do. We are achieving some positive results.*

Coaching is an important part of managing a poor performer. It is important to bear in mind that if the learner had known how to do it, they would have been doing it in the first place. In your coaching, you need not just to encourage them to identify what they need to do but you must also support them in learning how.

What if someone does not respond to being coached by their manager?

Most people respond well to being coached. but this is not always the case. Generally a reluctance to be coached may arise for one or more of the following reasons:

The individual is unwilling to admit there is scope for improvement, either in this instance or in general. In that case you must try to identify the barriers and deal with them. Reluctance to accept the need for improvement may arise from insecurity, so you should try to boost the person's confidence and give them encouragement. You should take every possible opportunity to give immediate, positive feedback to encourage the employee to adopt a more open mind-set towards being coached.

The individual may be reluctant to be coached by their manager because of past difficulties or perhaps because there is a major difference of style. The first step is to attempt to bury the hatchet and repair the relationship. Feelings will need to be discussed explicitly and differences in style accepted. It must be stressed that coaching is not evaluation.

A great impediment to coaching is the pressure of time and getting the job done. At least superficially it can appear that a 'tell them' approach is quicker. In the long run that is not the case: even in the short run, a job that needs to be repeated or repaired is not a quicker one. Managers I have spoken to who are highly trained and experienced in the skills of coaching are less likely to give in to these pressures, probably because they are more aware of the ultimate benefits of a coaching approach as opposed to a directive one.

It is also difficult to coach someone who mistrusts the organisation, as the boxed example illustrates.

I carried out an employee opinion survey for a firm of accountants. They were experiencing a high staff turnover, especially amongst the newly qualified accountants, and morale was low. The firm was also having difficulty recruiting the calibre of people it wanted.

In carrying out this survey, which involved both a questionnaire and one-to-one interviews, I found many problems. In particular, I found that in this command-and-control environment there was insufficient dialogue within the firm, whether this was about 'big-picture' issues or matters that affected people individually. In such a culture, it was not surprising to find that people were inherently uncomfortable about giving feedback.

In theory, the firm had a formal system whereby trainees would receive feedback on completion of an audit assignment. This was specifically part of their learning contract. The feedback should have been given to them by the 'senior' or 'manager' in charge of the audit. Most trainees complained that they never received this feedback. Consequently many had no idea what they had done well, or what they needed to improve on or do differently. They felt their development was impeded and that their only way of learning was to raise an issue with their external course tutor.

An organisational climate such as the one described here is not conducive to frank and open feedback sessions. A manager working in such a climate can, nonetheless, create a different culture within a team. An absolute requirement is the need to convince employees that frank and honest feedback will not be used against them. Particular effort must be put into giving real-time feedback, and into encouraging team members to use coaching styles upwards and among themselves. A climate of trust and sharing must be created within the team.

Values and beliefs are important. A non-directive model of coaching only works if you believe that people learn this way and also believe in the importance of continuous improvement and continuous learning.

How can an organisation encourage managers to adopt a coaching style of leadership?

In the last chapter we looked at the characteristics of organisations that have a discernible coaching culture. We saw that even where a coaching culture is well-embedded, by no means all managers use a coaching style of management. The reverse is equally true. There are many manager-coaches working in command-and-control cultures. Some of these organisations are likely to retain centralised command-and-control structures, at least in the near future. Others may evolve into coaching cultures.

The pressures we identified in the previous chapter that are driving some organisations to develop a coaching culture are causing others to recognise that new leadership styles are needed. There is a growing realisation that poor management is at the root of high staff turnover. As we saw, organisations are also waking up to the need for succession planning to ensure they are growing their future leaders from within. Diversity issues are also causing people to look at their management style, as is the management of younger people, often referred to as Generation X.

Generation X workers have a different mentality from their predecessors. They do not appreciate making the coffee and carrying the bags but seek more development and more opportunity, faster. Managing highly paid professionals and specialists also demands a more nuanced style of management. To help bring about a greater emphasis on managing and developing people, many organisations are introducing performance management and reward systems that underpin the values and behaviours they seek.

The HR manager of a large financial services company describes it like this:

The manager's role as a coach has been significantly underestimated and ignored. Everyone has been so busy doing the technical parts of the role. You cannot leave it to chance to expect the managers to manage the people. We have redesigned performance management and reward processes to build in an element of review and reward for people skills. We started with leadership behaviours, then broadened it. A proportion of an individual's bonus will be determined by how they live the company behaviours. There will also be a proportion of the bonus that is dependent on achieving people management goals, such as effectively carrying through performance management, managing poor performance and high performance and agreeing personal development plans for each member of the team. It will not be possible to say, 'I don't have time for this.' Managers will be required to discuss what won't get done, while they prioritise managing people.

What difficulties may the manager-coach experience in a command-and-control organisation?

Command-and-control management does not always fit easily with the whole notion of coaching and can create tension, especially when a manager-coach has a directive manager and, even more, if the two do not get on very well. This point is important to make because two people working together but deploying very different management styles are quite likely to experience tensions in their relationship. One will find the other's, inevitably more time-consuming, approach frustrating, while there will be an inevitable impatience the other way with an approach that is felt to be less effective in the long term. Tensions are also likely to be common in organisations that are in the throes of changing their leadership styles.

Two manager-coaches who work in command-and-control style financial services organisations describe their experiences. Both these managers had attended coaching skills for managers training programmes some 12 months previously. The first explained:

There are many downsides and impediments to using a coaching style of management in our style of organisation. The lines of authority in our small team are not clearly defined. Theoretically I am responsible for two juniors, but our manager has such a 'hands-on' style that he seldom delegates full control or responsibility to me. He often directs work to members in our team and I am kept out of the loop. This makes it very difficult to manage and assess them.

But there is another side to the coin: we are so very busy that it is not always possible for me to be involved in every project that my 'juniors' perform. It is a difficult situation either way.

To aggravate matters, some members of our department were disenchanted with our assessment process, which seemed to have little effect on promotions at the end of the year. People who had been highly rated were nonetheless passed over for promotion, and they felt this was because they did not work for powerful managers. This reduced the effectiveness of the whole performance appraisal process. It also seriously undermines you as a manager-coach.

Despite these problems, I am pleased I had the training. I have learned a great deal in the year following the course and because of it. Some of the learning that I have found the most valuable, and that I use the most, relates to how different individuals are motivated. Through the training, I have also gained a great deal more confidence in delegating work.

My feedback to my team members has improved, and I try to have feedback sessions with them on a more regular basis. I had always preferred to encourage rather than focus on individual weaknesses, but I have recognised that a few team members prefer a more direct approach and respond better when given constructive, 'real-time' feedback.

I gained more confidence in giving appraisals to poor performers, which I always found difficult. I find a coaching style much more effective than telling people what to do.

The other manager who attended the training programme is also convinced that a coaching style is a more effective way of managing people:

As a result of the course, I have completely changed style, for the better. Previously, I instinctively told people what they should do and how. I thought this was being assertive but through the training came to realise it did not help them to do the work on their own.

My boss has a strongly 'command-and-control' style, and his instinct is to tell me what to do. I try to get him to use a more coaching style, but he is not a good listener and he imposes his own views too much. He has had 360-degree feedback, which was consistent with my view of him. I coach him and try and get him to coach me, but it is hard-going. People like him have a different set of beliefs about how people behave and they will only change their approach if they can be persuaded of a different set of beliefs.

The organisation is process-oriented and results-driven, not a relationship environment. Everyone knows their job and gets on with it, with ever-decreasing resources and increasing profits. The people management style is that 'We are top-calibre people, we are clear about priorities, there is good communication, and a let's-get-on-with-it approach. In spite of that, if you need help it is there, and I do get recognition for being a good manager-coach. I am always allocated graduate trainees, and it is recognised that graduate trainees become effective more quickly with me. I write my own appraisal objectives each year, and I always include people goals and developing others.

I always give recognition to my staff and work hard to make sure they don't fail. Their good work and results are always recognised by my manager in my appraisal.

The experiences of these two managers illustrate some difficulties of being a manager-coach with a command-and-control boss. Nonetheless, both cases show individuals who remain committed to a coaching style of management despite everything, and are both convinced that it helps them to manage more effectively even in a less supportive environment. Their commitment is, however, made possible by two critical factors. First, even though they are working in a command-and-control environment, they receive recognition for their effectiveness as coaches, and for the results they achieve through coaching. Secondly, they have complete control over their work, setting their own objectives, priorities and timescales. If these factors are absent, I would fear that the philosophy clash might be too great and cause the manager-coach to revert to a command-and-control style.

A complementary question is whether a coaching style used by some individual managers can be disruptive to a command-and-control organisation. I believe this is indeed likely to be the case, unless there is some encouragement from the top, or some form of reward or recognition. Difficulties are especially likely to arise in the smaller, owner-managed business. Some years back, I worked as an HR adviser to a small, family business where the directors (all family members) were hands-on, command-and-control managers, whereas two of the senior managers were natural coaches. Clashes were frequent, staff felt they were being pulled in different directions and discontent arose.

How can we develop managers to be coaches?

To become a manager-coach, the individual needs to hold beliefs that are consonant with those required for being an effective coach, namely, that learning is important and that a coaching style enables people to learn better and perform better. They need to be clear about the competencies required to be a successful manager-coach . They also need a good level of self-awareness about their preferred way of learning and the impact on others of their interpersonal and leadership style. Excellent communication skills are also essential.

Some approaches that I find helpful are to use diagnostic instruments, such as:

- the Strengths Deployment Inventory,[4] which provides a framework for managing relationships and assessing how your interpersonal style impacts on others
- the honey and Mumford Learning Styles Questionnaire,[5] which enables individuals to identify their preferred way of learning
- situational Leadership (Hersey and Blanchard),[6] which works extremely effectively in helping people identify how to adapt their leadership style to suit how willing, committed and experienced the employee is to perform the particular task
- 360-degree feedback which, based on how the individual learner performs against the organisation's competency profile or desired leadership competencies, is also helpful.

It goes without saying that training in the key coaching skills of active listening, giving real-time feedback, setting goals and reflecting are essential.

There are many other diagnostic instruments, areas of knowledge and skills that might be covered. The ones you use should suit the needs of the individual learner and the circumstances of the organisation.

The depth and breadth of the development required will also depend on whether the organisation has a coaching culture, or is aiming to move towards one. In the latter case, a combined management development and coaching programme will be required (see Chapter 7). Where coaching is already well embedded and where there are sufficient role models and encouragement from the top, people may require minimal training or development to become a manager-coach. Where an individual's beliefs are not consonant with those required of a coach, this person may require one-to-one coaching.

KEY LEARNING POINTS

Coaching is an effective style of management and is more suited to the leadership and people management challenges facing managers in today's working environment.

To be an effective manager-coach you need to be able to adapt your style to suit the individual and the circumstances.

Ideally, coaching should be a normal way of doing things in a team. Opportunities to coach crop up constantly and do not need to be set up. Managers should also use coaching techniques to help individuals get the most from on-the-job learning.

The manager-coach needs to give real-time feedback to individuals, and should create opportunities that enable staff to broaden skills and take on additional responsibilities.

Coaching is also effective for helping poor performers raise their levels of performance and for enhancing learning and development for good and high performers.

Manager-coaches are likely to find tensions in a command-and-control organisation or with a command-and-control boss. Manager-coaches can achieve effective results even in these circumstances, though they should ideally receive encouragement and recognition for their management style.

A combined training and coaching programme, one-to-one coaching or having effective role models within the organisation are different ways of helping managers develop a coaching style. The development techniques and tools used will vary according to the individual's needs and organisational circumstances.

Diagnostic instruments that provide a focus for understanding how to develop effective relationship management, leadership and learning styles may be helpful.

Communication skills training is also likely to be required.

NOTES AND REFERENCES

1   © Janice Caplan, 2003.

2   CHARTERED INSTITUTE OF PERSONNEL AND DEVELOPMENT (2002) *Who Learns at Work?* London, CIPD. March.

3   GIBBS G. (1998) *Learning by Doing: A guide to teaching and learning methods.* London, FEU Longmans.

4   PERSONAL STRENGTHS PUBLISHING *The Strengths Deployment Inventory* Peterborough, PSP. Available at www.personalstrengths.co.uk.

5   HONEY P. *and* MUMFORD A. (2000) *Learning Styles Questionnaire.* Maidenhead, Peter Honey Publications.

6   HERSEY P. BLANCHARD K. H. *and* JOHNSON D. E. (2000) *Management of Organisational Behaviour: Leading Human Resources.* 8th edn. New Jersey, Prentice Hall.

3

Executive coaching

One-to-one executive coaching has become hugely popular in the last few years. It offers a unique opportunity for managers and executives to engage in a personally tailored programme designed to accelerate professional development or enhance performance.

Executive coaching is about bringing out the best in people and conveying them from where they are now to where they want to be. It is a highly personalised learning process that is tailored to the learner's knowledge base, learning style and pace. It raises self-awareness, uncovers blind spots and enables the executive to accomplish more than otherwise he or she would have.

The literature on leadership development and on learning shows that to develop real leaders, organisations need to provide guided leadership experience, help people learn from their mistakes, give them challenging assignments in their career and provide extensive mentoring and time for reflection. Few organisations succeed at doing this. As Robert Witherspoon,[1] a coach and acknowledged expert in the field points out, 'Most organisations do not breed leaders. Most are poor teachers of leadership, and few are organised to develop real leaders . . . A coach can be of enormous help in this on-going process.'

The questions I will be looking at in this chapter are: When is it appropriate to use executive coaching, and for whom? What are the different types of coaching that are available? What are the differences between them?

WHEN IS IT APPROPRIATE TO USE EXECUTIVE COACHING, AND FOR WHOM?

Executive coaching programmes are usually change- or growth-oriented. They are a valuable learning solution for the following people and the following situations:

- Executives who are leading significant organisational change efforts.
- Executives who are positioned for promotion. In these cases, coaching needs to be part of a wider plan that will also include broad organisational exposure or bigger job assignments.
- Executives who wish to develop their career paths and promotional prospects or who are experiencing obstacles to their advancement.

- Executives who need to keep up with the pace of change or have reached a career plateau. All executives need to keep learning and developing so as to keep up with change in their operating environment. Rapid change can quickly compromise an organisation's ability to compete. Executives have two different sets of pressures here. One is the rate of learning required to keep them ahead in their own specialism. The other is the rate of learning required in other, broader disciplines. All executives give priority to their own specialism. Having a coach to support their learning in other areas can be both time- and effort-effective.

- Coaching is valuable in helping newly appointed executives develop into their roles. If someone is taking on a management role for the first time, or if the new role is considerably larger than the previous one, the individual can benefit from a skilled coach to help come to grips with their responsibilities.

- 360-degree feedback, where an individual receives feedback on behaviour from subordinates and peers, as well as his or her 'manager', is gaining in popularity. Coaching is effective in helping people understand the feedback and work on the ensuing development plans.

- Executives who are experiencing job stress or interpersonal conflicts benefit from coaching. There is a close connection between an executive's behaviour and business success. A skilled coach can help facilitate adjustments in behaviour.

- Coaching is frequently used to help executives improve the balance between work and life demands. Many organisations are recognising that rapid change, downsizing and the long-hours culture create significant stress for executives. Coaching can be a way of helping the executive relieve stress and achieve a better balance between work and home. Coaching in these circumstances is often motivational.

- Coaching helps executives deal more effectively with change. Individuals working in organisations that are going through culture or structural changes need to make adjustments to their behaviour. A coach can help the person make these adjustments. Many say coaching provides insights about their leadership and better understanding of their impact on the team.

- Coaching can also be an effective, and sometimes essential, way of helping implement a diversity programme. Coaching helps people value and appreciate diversity. It is also immensely valuable in supporting women and people from racial and other minorities who work in a predominantly white, male organisation.

- Similarly, coaching is also gaining recognition as an effective tool for helping people work together, or manage others across geographic, cultural or demographic boundaries.

- The old saying 'It is lonely at the top' is very true. The higher your position in the organisation, the less likely you are to receive honest feedback. Greater visibility is accompanied by higher levels of scrutiny. An executive's decisions become increasingly pivotal and mistakes prove more costly. An experienced coach fills the gap by providing frank, objective support and feedback.

- In the quest for innovation and creativity, organisations need to encourage individuality and better teamworking at one and the same time. In such circumstances, a coach can give an individual the opportunity to sound out and think through ideas without inadvertently creating disquiet among their team.

- Anecdotal evidence indicates that team coaching is gaining in popularity. It may be used to help build the team, improve group dynamics in the boardroom or among executive groups, or to help the members of the team come to grips with changes.

Coaching is also a powerful technique for guiding people who are experiencing problems. For example:

- for a long-serving executive who has previously performed satisfactorily but is now having difficulties with a new manager/the new culture/the new way of doing things

- in organisations where, until recently, managers have been judged on their ability to manage the product but are now being measured on their ability to manage people. Not only has the organisation invested heavily in these people, these people for their part have invested their commitment and lives in the organisation. Support to make the change without this being counted against them is a sensible investment decision on both sides.

- where an organisation is to be sold or taken over, the incumbent management may be keen to retain the knowledge of existing managers and staff but want them to adapt to the new culture and way of doing things quickly. Coaching may enable the change to be achieved relatively painlessly.

- where an executive's interpersonal skills are a cause of dissatisfaction among the staff. In the familiar set-up, the individual's foibles may be tolerated, perhaps fondly, but a new management may view the individual less kindly.

Until recently, coaching was used mainly for individuals who were having problems. The change in emphasis and perspective to coaching as a tool for development is to be welcomed. It signals the benefits coaching can achieve in a wider range of circumstances. More importantly, it indicates a sea change in attitudes about leaders and leadership. It recognises that leadership is not about knowing all the answers but about learning. It recognises that leaders are not organisational superheroes but people with different strengths and weaknesses and gaps in their knowledge.

WHAT IS THE ROLE OF THE COACH?

These many and varied reasons for executive coaching give rise to some subtle differences in the type of coaching that is required.

Witherspoon, referred to above, has set out a typology of executive coaching that is both comprehensive and extremely useful. He classifies four executive coaching roles on a continuum – see Figure 6 on page 37.

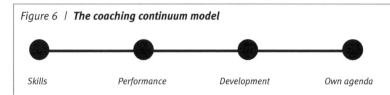

Figure 6 | ***The coaching continuum model***

Skills   Performance   Development   Own agenda

An understanding of the distinctions between these different coaching roles is especially helpful to the HR manager. It provides a framework for identifying when coaching is an appropriate solution, for selecting a coach and for helping the executive identify their learning needs. Witherspoon himself uses these distinctions with his clients in jointly setting the coaching agenda. 'Unless my client and I can identify one of these coaching roles as primary, there can be confusion about expectations, the amount of time it will take and the effort we will put into the relationship.' These distinctions also help ensure that the coaching remains focused on its goals, with an end point clearly identified. This is essential for ensuring that the coaching achieves something and is not just nice to have.

Witherspoon's continuum is invaluable for enhancing our understanding of coaching and how we use it. I would like to see it universally adopted. The following descriptions and analysis are set against the continuum and are based on my own experience and on the extensive input I have received from many executive coaches, all of whom are acknowledged in the introduction to this book.

Coaching for skills

Skills coaching focuses on a learner's current project, task or activity. It provides quick help to someone to learn a new skill, or build on existing ones. The need for skill-building may be recognised directly by the individual, or it may have been identified through a formal assessment process, such as performance appraisal or a 360-feedback exercise. Examples of such skills coaching may be public speaking, selection interviewing, performance appraisal, public relations, how to cold-call, product knowledge and so on.

In this type of coaching, the executive learns specific skills, abilities and perspectives, usually over a short time. The skills to be learned are likely to be clear from the start. The coach performs an assessment of the learner's needs, and discusses the results with the learner. Coach and learner work together to draw up a learning plan and carry it through. Skills coaching tends to be brief and circumscribed. When the executive learns the skill, the coaching is finished. Skills coaching is distinct from training or teaching, which rely on the trainer telling, instructing and showing. Rather, skills coaching is a dialogue focused around observation, enquiry and discovery. It is about facilitating and helping the executive learn.

The skills coach needs to be a specialist in the subject at hand, as well, of course, as being a skilled coach.

Coaching for performance

This form of coaching focuses on the executive's effectiveness in his or her current position. Performance standards are often related to a competency profile, and the need for performance coaching may be identified through a 360-degree review, performance appraisal or from some other measure such as staff turnover. Performance coaching may be arranged for a newly appointed executive, or an executive whose role is changing, or it may be part of a leadership development training programme to help the individual transfer the classroom learning to the workplace. It may also be 'corrective' and involve interventions to remedy problems that are interfering with an executive's performance and that may also risk derailing the executive.

Performance coaching is more comprehensive than skills coaching in that it looks at the impact of the learner's personal style on work effectiveness. It too begins with an assessment, and this assessment is likely to seek input from a wide range of sources.

Performance coaching is usually spread over an extended period. Specific, work-oriented goals are set. The focus might be on the executive's competencies. Examples are analytical skills or tasks, such as problem-solving measures, team-building or operations management.

The performance coach must be skilled and experienced in the area in which they are providing coaching and may also bring in other experts when required. To be credible, the coach will probably also need to be at the same level or status as the learner.

Coaching for development

Coaching for development helps prepare an executive for a new career step or for future assignments and responsibilities.

There are two typical scenarios that development coaching might cover. One scenario is where it is hard to predict the precise competencies that will be required for a future role, as these change rapidly. This often occurs where the coaching is part of succession planning. In this scenario, the coaching typically focuses on helping the learner discover strengths and weaknesses, determine where growth is needed and how to fill the gaps. Helping the learner learn how to learn is an important element of development coaching in this scenario.

The second scenario is often referred to as career coaching and is about helping the person identify their career aspirations and plans. In such cases, career coaches provide expert feedback, advice and guidance on career and work–life decisions, career transitions and related activities.

Where the skills, knowledge and behaviours required for the next step are clearly identified, development coaching focuses on the gap between the learner's current skills, capabilities and knowledge and where the learner is aiming to be.

Coaching for the executive's agenda

This type of coaching is much more open-ended than the others. Usually, the learner's own goals for the coaching will be linked to the achievement of wider business goals.

Coaching for performance is about working with someone to increase their effectiveness in their current job. Coaching to the executive's agenda involves working on larger issues, including obtaining better business results. In this type of coaching, we are looking at highly personalised learning. Each person has a unique knowledge base, learning pace and learning style. Executive agenda coaching can uncover blind spots and change someone's style. Personal aspects of our lives do not stay out of our working lives. Everyone brings to their work every aspect of themselves: their personality, thoughts, attitudes, values, behaviours, habits, needs, wants and fears. This type of coaching may take this 'holistic' view of someone and is more likely to include personal goals than other forms of coaching.

Executive agenda coaching is usually aimed at senior-ranking executives and is likely to last for an extended period. The coach may be available on a regular basis or as needed. The coach may also help the learner think things through, reflect, make decisions and provide support when problems get difficult or the process gets lonely. The coach can act as a sounding board and reality test.

Coaching to the executive's agenda may include career coaching, performance coaching and skill-building and, in such cases, there will be a 'lead coach' who will call in other specialist coaches. In drawing up the learner's coaching plan, coach and learner may identify that the learner needs help with personal issues such as financial planning, and the coach may bring in advisers to help the learner on these matters.

THE COACHING PROCESS

We have seen from the above descriptions that the coaching role may differ according to the individual's needs and circumstances. The process, however, always follows the same stages:

- analysis of where the learner is now
- identification of coaching goals and finalisation of the coaching plan
- implementation of the plan
- evaluation of success.

EXAMPLES OF THE FOUR TYPES OF COACHING

The following examples illustrate each stage of the coaching process for all four coaching roles and show how these may be subtly different.

Coaching for skills

Analysis

In skills coaching, the analysis is likely to be performed through observation of the learner in action.

Some years back, I was engaged by Shelley Stock Hutter, a firm of accountants, to coach their senior partners for presentations they were to make at a breakfast seminar for clients and prospective clients.

We started the session by discussing their concerns and then each partner delivered a presentation. We video-recorded them, played back the tape and critiqued their performance.

Goals

With coaching for skills, the goals are almost always readily evident. The coach employs their experience and perhaps some formal techniques to ascertain the existing skill level of the learner and develops an expert idea of the end result needed. The coaching will focus on getting to that end result.

Continuing with the presentations skills coaching example, we identified each person's goals easily by comparing their 'live' recording against our expert ideas of public speaking. This enabled each person to draw up a coaching plan. For example, one person needed to work on the content of her presentation; another needed to work on mannerisms and eye contact.

Implementation

The learners were coached as a team. This was more cost-effective for them but it also meant that the seminar was created as a whole rather than as a set of separate presentations. Presentations and delivery styles were arranged to complement one another and provide variety.

In coaching the partners, I encouraged them to provide input on their own performance and identify what they did well or not well. I then facilitated and gave feedback based around their needs. This is radically different from a training programme, where they would have been instructed in techniques.

Evaluation

The presentations were enthusiastically reviewed and the firm now runs these seminars on a regular basis. We were able to conclude that the coaching had achieved the desired outcome.

Coaching for performance

Analysis

In performance coaching, data will be collected about the learner's current performance and their impact on others and on the business. Common sources of data are 360-degree feedback, employee opinion surveys, performance appraisals, a training course, talking to any other party involved in the coaching, such as the learner's line manager, etc. Which sources data is taken from will depend on circumstances, such as the availability of existing data and the learner's own suggestions, preferences, aims and levels of self-awareness.

By way of illustration, I recently performed three coaching assignments in the same organisation. The learners and their circumstances were so different that I used different methods of analysis for each. For one, we carried out a 360-degree feedback exercise based on a specially designed competency profile. This enabled the learner to understand better how people from different backgrounds perceived his performance. For another, I conducted an opinion survey and interviewed the staff and peers with whom he worked closely. This learner already had a high level of self-awareness as regards his behaviour but wished to know what his staff felt about his business strategies and how he ran his department. For the third we used self-analysis data he had collected on a recent training programme and some confidential reports from his line manager and chief executive. This learner had a very high self-awareness, supported by existing data, and a clear idea of the issues he needed to address.

Goals

In performance coaching, goals are often set with reference to a competency profile or to other organisational measures, or to business plans and strategies.

One of the above-mentioned learners managed a cross-cultural engineering team, based in three different continents. We set goals in reference to his business plan and to the company's global plan. We identified communication and teamwork as needing to be improved and drew up the coaching plan around the behaviours critical to success and how he could adopt, role-model and roll these out across the team.

Implementation

I designed the coaching programme for this learner to fit in with his travel schedule, identifying action points and independent learning that were relevant to each forthcoming business trip. There were eight sessions, extended over one year.

In another coaching assignment, the learner's agenda was to improve relationships with some of his colleagues. We ran four sessions in as many weeks. By talking through examples of when he had been aggressive and what he could have said instead, the learner identified ways of changing his style to be more collaborative, and to be assertive and decisive rather than aggressive. Once he had acquired these behaviours, the challenge was to find ways of keeping this going under stress. We achieved this by running two follow-up sessions at monthly intervals, and I also made sure the learner would be able to telephone at any time to talk issues through and discuss the appropriate behaviours.

Evaluation

Measurement of results flows naturally from the setting of the initial coaching objectives. These need to be clear and specific and relate to the individual's personal objectives, which in turn should link to business objectives.

In the last example given above, the new behaviour became embedded and the learner received promotion, fulfilling both his own and the company's goals.

In the cross-cultural example, the learner produced a reflective report for his chief executive setting out the personal and business objectives he had achieved through the coaching. A further measure of success came a short while later through analysis of business results.

Coaching for development

Analysis

The data needed for development coaching varies according to the scenario and may rely on sources such as those used for performance coaching, or may involve the learner's participation in an assessment or development centre programme.

Many of the organisations studied for this book have a team of career coaches who are available for anyone who wishes to access them to take stock of their career and to identify a career path. This is particularly so in professional service firms where career development coaching is provided for those at qualified and 'manager' level. For these people, the next step is partnership, but only if they can meet stringent requirements.

At KPMG, for example, the requirements for being made a partner are well-defined and individuals attend a career development centre, or similar meeting where their skills and capabilities are identified and an action plan is drawn up.

Goals

In development coaching, goals may be set with reference to the requirements of the next role or assignment. Identifying the skills, knowledge and key behaviours required for different roles may be a critical part of the coaching process. Equipping the learner to continue learning in order to keep up with changes to career paths and to jobs is a critical goal in development coaching.

In firms such as KPMG, where the next role is clearly identified, the coaching goals will focus on the areas identified in the assessment centre in which the learner is weak or lacks the experience required for the position.

In other cases, where the career path or the next role is less well defined, the coaching will focus on finding out what options are open to the learner and how they can prepare themselves. The coaching in these circumstances might call for a clear-sighted look at how realistic the learner's aspirations are.

Implementation

The coach then works with the learner on refining their goals and following through on the action plan. Specialist coaches may be introduced, or the learner may attend training, work on special projects or gain structured experience in another job, as well as receiving coaching support and challenge.

Many organisations set up arrangements for junior people to be mentored by more senior people in the organisation. Mentoring arrangements encourage the learner to learn more about the organisation and keep up with developments. This helps them identify possible career paths and plan the learning and experience they need to get there.

Coaching to the executive's own agenda

Analysis

In executive agenda coaching, data will be collected from an even wider range of sources and may take longer to assemble. It is likely to involve the learner in taking fresh psychometric or diagnostic tests, even if these have been undergone in the past.

Many executive agenda coaches spend a day with the learner, initially, to determine goals, develop the psychological contract and agree on process. Many conduct this initial day off-site and use leisure facilities to oil the relationship and help both parties get to know one another.

There are several subjects and situations the executive coach usually taps into. The coach looks at how the executive behaves as part of the team, at their impact as the leader of the team, at what their leadership philosophy is, how visible they are and feel they should be, and at how they handle themselves emotionally. They may raise work–life balance issues. They will create a safe environment that enables the learner to develop new perspectives and explore ideas which they might previously have dismissed.

Much effort goes into appraising where the executive is now in terms of leadership and interpersonal styles, thinking patterns and so on, using diverse psychometric instruments and 360-degree assessment.

Many executive coaches take a holistic view of the person and their lifestyle, and include in their initial analysis a review of the executive's whole lifestyle: health, children, finances and other personal matters.

At the heart of executive coaching lies the notion that everyone has a pattern of behaviour that is always changing. Many executive coaches spend time getting to know the learner's environment, so that they can have an understanding of how this shapes the learner's behaviour. They can then help the learner both adapt to and shape that environment.

Goals

Once the initial analysis has been carried out, the coach and learner then draw up a coaching plan and identify the business deliverables. When coaching to the executive's agenda, the goal-setting process is often less clear than with the other coaching roles, and several different reference points are sought. The goals set may be short- and long-term ones. For example, Robert Craven coaches owner-managers of small businesses. One learner's end goal was to grow his business. To achieve this, the learner needed to implement painful and difficult decisions. These gave rise to the shorter-term goals of the coaching. Bob Garratt, who coaches main board directors of large companies, agrees four high-level business goals with each learner. These might be adjusting to a new job, driving strategic change or making a major presentation.

It is the role of the coach to work with the learner to identify the performance levels that will provide them with a very good chance of getting there. These lower-level goals usually remain confidential between coach and learner. They may be personal and they are often about removing barriers to successful performance. For example, Garratt cites one learner who had financial anxieties that adversely affected his work performance. Sometimes the barriers are behavioural and require an attitude shift, as in a situation described by executive coach Ros Taylor regarding a learner who was technically brilliant but seen as a bully.

Implementation

Implementation methods almost always include 'homework' assignments in which the learner tries something different or gathers feedback.

Own-agenda coaching often involves more than one coach. In such cases, there is likely to be a 'lead' coach who may bring in others to advise and assist, for example, with the financial review, or as a voice coach, or to deal with the individual's personal appearance.

Other ways in which the coaching is implemented may vary considerably from coach to coach. Some coaches accompany their learners to meetings so that they can observe their behaviour directly.

In all cases, it is the coaching discussion that is the most important. This can depend, critically, on the coach's ability to listen, question, challenge, understand and build confidence.

Coaching assignments are likely to vary considerably in duration. Some may extend over a few months; others may run for over a year. The length of sessions also varies from one hour to one day, though the latter is usually for learners who fly in from overseas.

Evaluation

As with the other coaching roles, success is measured on the basis of achievement of the goals, both business and personal, identified at the outset.

When coaching doesn't work and how to avoid this

When arranging executive coaching, the organisation needs to be clear and specific about the desired business results and should negotiate these with the people to be coached. One coach tells how a learner clearly used her as an 'ego-trip'. The coaching goals had been agreed between coach and learner but not with the organisation.

It is important for the learner to be committed before the start. Another coach tells of one uncommitted learner who was passive throughout and who never completed the action points agreed at the sessions. He was clearly just going through the motions to satisfy his bosses.

The organisation should recognise that coaching is a confidential process and not seek feedback from the coach about an individual. One coach tells how she was called in by a learner's manager and asked for her view on how effective a manager the learner was and if he was suitable for promotion.

It is also important to be sure that the goalposts do not change during the coaching and that unrealistic pressures are not put on the employee. In one case, the business's new owners decided to move the learner overseas against his will. Indications are they had made this decision before signing off the coaching and the coaching goals.

KEY LEARNING POINTS

Organisations are using coaching to help executives learn, develop, improve their performance, build their skills and take on new roles and responsibilities.

Coaching roles can be divided into four different categories: coaching for skills, for performance, for development and to the executive's agenda. These distinctions are helpful in determining the expectations of the coaching, the nature of the intervention, the time it will take and the level of effort required by the learner. For the HR practitioner it is a useful framework against which to select a coach and manage coaching relationships across the organisation.

These different coaching roles all work to the same process, to which there are four stages: analysis of needs, setting of coaching goals, implementation of coaching and evaluation of success. There are subtle differences in each of these stages across the four coaching roles.

Over the next few chapters I look at different ways that executive coaching can be used to achieve strategic business goals. In the second part of the book, I discuss the ins and outs of managing the whole coaching process as an HR practitioner.

NOTES AND REFERENCES

1   WITHERSPOON R. (2000) 'Starting smart: clarifying coaching goals and rules' in GOLDSMITH M., LYONS L. *and* FREAS A. (eds) *Coaching for Leadership.* San Francisco, Jossey-Bass Pfeiffer.

4

Implementing a coaching programme

I wish to turn now to look at how different organisations use one-to-one coaching to achieve their strategic aims. In the following case studies, I examine different programmes and what they achieve, drawing lessons from them so that HR practitioners can relate the studies to their own situations.

In each case study, I set out to answer three principal questions: What business goals have they been designed to meet? How are these programmes implemented? How do they fit into the culture and processes of the organisation?

Coaching the BBC Newsgathering team

What are the business reasons for introducing coaching?

In recent years, live reporting and 24-hour broadcasting have brought significant changes to the way the news is presented to us by the mainstream television channels. The style has moved from a presenter standing in front of a building to some spectacular, highly imaginative shots. These changes have demanded new skills of the television reporters, and especially the reporters who bring us live coverage. At the same time competition has intensified, as viewers now have access to a wider choice of channels.

To keep ahead in such a climate, reporters need to update and improve their skills continuously. The BBC Newsgathering team finds that one-to-one coaching is a highly effective way of enabling them to do this. They have two coaches on the team: one, Carla Hargis, who coaches reporters on their delivery skills, and the other, Fiona Anderson, who coaches on how the journalists write and package their broadcasts.

The coaching that Hargis and Anderson provide also meets needs that arise from other causes. Journalistic training rarely, if ever, includes live reporting. While some people receive guidance when they first enter news broadcasting they are then left to sink or swim. Related to this, some broadcasters of many years' standing do not realise their style has become outdated or that they have acquired personal mannerisms that may grate with viewers.

Secondly, the pace of television news is frenetic. As soon as the report is done, it's old news, and it's on to the next piece. Such a fast-moving environment is not conducive to reflection and feedback on performance. Hargis and Anderson make up for this lacuna, as their sessions are opportunities for people to receive feedback and analyse how they do things.

How is the coaching implemented?

Hargis believes anyone can learn live skills. It depends on whether they are willing to practise. The BBC encourages every reporter to have at least one coaching session on writing and one on presentation every year. Sometimes people have more or have follow-up sessions a few months later.

When coaching was first introduced some people were defensive and thought the coaching was a punishment, but they quickly came to see it is a benefit and a way to develop skills; it provides an opportunity to experiment without being on-air. The coaching is now oversubscribed, and the vast majority of reporters are grateful for the two hours or so of someone focusing on them and their development.

Hargis and Anderson are skills coaches who see their role as being to get people to think, 'What is my own way, my style, my uniqueness? What am I saying? How am I connecting with the audience? What is the message behind what I am saying?'

Analysing the individual's learning needs and setting the coaching goals

In the previous chapter, we saw that the skills coach must have a clear idea of the standards that the learner needs to reach. Hargis and Anderson are familiar with these from their research, their experience and from the BBC's plans and policies. But also, in this environment, standards are constantly discussed both formally and informally in the newsroom: the reporters themselves are highly self-critical and, as dedicated professionals, are striving to maintain and improve performance.

Hargis has researched extensively into the latest techniques of live reporting, and she works with learners on these. She coaches them on all aspects of delivery, such as how they use their voice to inject a sense of immediacy into breaking news stories. She aims to enable people to show their true personality and to be animating. Hargis is careful not to instruct and only becomes directive where the learner is unable to identify their needs and solutions, when she makes sure to explain her reasoning and the supporting research. Hargis puts across most coaching points by viewing with the learner their own recordings and a range of videotapes of other reporters, comparing these with their own reports and encouraging them to identify characteristics they think are important and can incorporate into their own style.

Anderson aims to get people to be authentic and credible. She coaches them on working with pictures and sound, creating a clear story-flow with a logical structure, using interviews and other techniques to carry the story forward. Anderson also views their videotapes with learners and encourages them to criticise their reports by asking them questions such as, 'Why did you put that there?' Anderson feels much of her work lies in confidence-building and encouraging people to become more practised so that they do not lose critical skills in the heat of the battle. Anderson coaches to standards that she is able to identify as an 'expert'. She also draws on *The Reporter's Friend*, a book written by Vin Ray, the Executive Editor and Deputy Head of Newsgathering, based on his experience and used widely by BBC reporters. Most importantly, Anderson refers extensively to audience research. For example, she has recently completed an audience research project on the BBC's reporting of the developing world and has produced a training video based on the findings.

As well as issues such as these of style and technique, Hargis and Anderson often work with learners on attitude and approach. For example:

- They encourage people to take risks. Many reporters, who have achieved a role with BBC Television News against enormous competition, feel they must play it safe. They think they must conform to a supposed BBC way of doing things which they identify as formal. Hargis and Anderson emphasise that the BBC needs a variety of styles if it is to appeal to a wide audience.

- Many reporters are often overly self-critical and focused on perfection, castigating themselves if their tie is crooked or they stumble on a word. Hargis works with them to get them to evaluate themselves as the viewer does. Hargis and Anderson often find they have to work hard to get learners to recognise what they do well.

- Anderson finds that reporters are often so familiar with a story they forget viewers may be hearing it for the first time and may need to hear about the context in order to understand fully why the latest development matters.

How is the coaching evaluated?

The senior management and programme editors measure the effectiveness of the coaching by what they see on air. Subjective assessment of 'indicators' is therefore minimised by direct assessment of the quality of output: if it is perceived to be improving then the coaching is self-evidently successful. Audience research is another indicator of how effective the coaching is, as is the continuing demand for coaching from the learners themselves.

Gaining acceptance

Acceptance of coaching within this organisation comes from a number of sources:

- The coaches are respected for their expertise and skills.

- The learners appreciate the opportunity they are being given.

- As far as possible the coaching is non-threatening. It is rare for the coaching to be corrective, though Hargis can recall a situation in the US where a reporter became so flustered during a live report she had to be taken off-air. She was coached and, after about a year, returned successfully to live broadcasts.

CASE STUDY continued

- There is complete confidentiality.

Both Hargis and Anderson feel that maintaining strict confidentiality is key to ensuring that coaching is acceptable and seen as developmental. They do not give feedback on what is discussed in the sessions, though managers are given reports in broad terms, to ensure the reporters get adequate support and encouragement as they work on changes.

How does the coaching fit into the culture and processes of the organisation?

It is important to achieve clarity and consistency between the coaching and other organisational messages. There are many ways in which this is achieved. When the coaching first started, Hargis spent considerable time with the editor discussing vision and strategy. Anderson was already a part of the team. Both Hargis and Anderson participate in away-day meetings and receive programme and audience research. They maintain a regular dialogue with the programme editors about standards to be sure everyone is working to the same ends. The Newsgathering team has a clear set of standards to work to, which are set at the highest possible level. Hargis and Anderson need to be consistent with this strategy and yet must allow for individual creativity. Anderson also works with producers and 'back of camera' people on various training workshops to ensure that consistent messages are being communicated to the whole team and that the reporters are not being 'coached' in isolation.

Lord Reith, the first Director General of the BBC, laid down a definition of the purpose of the BBC to 'inform, educate and entertain'; the word 'connect' has recently been added to these. This definition is an important reference point for setting standards in the newsroom, as are the development programmes established by the current Director General, Greg Dyke, 'Making it Happen' and 'Valuing People'. These are essentially about communicating the corporate strategy, vision and values throughout the BBC.

CASE STUDY 2

Coaching in sales-driven call centres

Call centre personnel respond to customer enquiries, problems and complaints by telephone.

Historically, sales-driven call centres have been seen solely as customer service centres rather than as revenue generators. But, in more recent years, businesses have realised that their call centre staff have a valuable one-to-one relationship with the customer and are often the main point of contact the customer has with the business. Call centre staff are therefore critical to the company's ability to retain customers and to cross-sell different services. They can have a powerful influence on a company's reputation, as well as having a direct impact on company profits. Many businesses, consequently, have been reassessing the role of their call centres and have sought to introduce a customer service ethos, using coaching as the key tool for achieving it.

What are the business reasons for introducing a coaching programme?

In some areas of the country it is difficult to recruit call centre staff, and many call centres suffer from a high turnover of staff. This difficulty is related to many different factors. Sometimes it is because the work attracts people who are looking to fill in time for a short while. Sometimes it is because the work is monotonous. Call centres are often highly regulated environments, where you have little control over your day. The calls come in, you take them and are closely supervised. Often there are limited career prospects.

Many call centres seem to suffer from at least one or more of these problems, and these often come across to the customer.

We have all had instances of listening to a recorded message offering assurance that you are moving up the queue. One of my business partners once spent an hour holding on for technical support to solve a problem he had encountered in installing some newly purchased software, only to have the person at the other end of the telephone hang up because he could not solve the problem (it turned out to be a fault with the program). Others have complained of uninterested and curt responses to their queries. I called up to make a general enquiry about medical insurance, only to have the person on the other end ask me extremely personal questions without first checking whether I was able to speak privately. In any event, these questions were unnecessary given the nature of my enquiry. Such incidents are a part of almost everyone's experience.

Many call centres have tried different ways of raising standards and increasing motivation. Mostly these ideas fall well short of attaining the desired results. The coaches and consultants featured in this chapter are convinced that well-constructed coaching programmes achieve far greater success than training courses, away-days and manuals of dos and don'ts.

How are customer service standards identified?

We have seen in previous chapters that for all skills coaching it is important to know the standards to which learners should aspire and against which they are to be assessed. As a starting point, therefore, those responsible for call centres need a clear idea of what they want to achieve and their priorities. While this is easy to state as an objective, getting consistent goals from line managers is often not so easy, because there are some difficult choices and dilemmas involved. For example, how important is customer satisfaction compared with staff productivity? Is an efficient call one that is completed quickly or one that answers all of the customer's problems?

Much greater success has been achieved by those call centres where the importance of creating a satisfied customer base is recognised. The staff are ideally sufficiently well engaged with the organisation that they become genuine advocates of its services, and satisfied customers report good experiences to their friends.

Customers generally have both declared and latent needs. The declared need is the reason they have called. The latent need is something they may not yet have recognised, perhaps because they are unaware the service is available, or perhaps because they have not made the connection between the service and its application to their particular circumstances. If the call centre can efficiently satisfy not only their customers' declared needs but also their latent needs, then they have delivered added value to the customers and created extra income for the company. This can build and sustain customer engagement and create a strong and enduring sense of attachment between the customer and the product or service.

Julia Blandford has worked with several organisations helping them revamp their call centres. She describes how, working with a large financial services organisation, they identified that they wanted to move a call centre agent–customer interaction from this kind of conversation, which satisfies only the customer's immediate need

A customer calls and says they want to check to see if a payment has been received. 'I sent a cheque last week; have you got it on my account yet?'
    The call centre agent checks and responds, 'Yes, we have received it. Goodbye.'

– to this kind of customer interaction, which satisfies the customer's declared and latent needs:

Call centre: 'Yes, we received it on the 18th. I can see from your account that you make this payment in full every month. Are you aware you can do this by direct debit?'

Answer: 'No – it sounds complicated.'

Call centre: 'It's very straightforward. We send you a notice at the beginning of the month, telling you what your monthly bill is, and then 14 days later we take that amount directly from your bank without you having to go to the trouble to write a cheque. You can stop using direct debit at any time. If you like, I can send you the details together with a form to set it up.'

The customer thinks about this for a moment and then says, 'Yes, OK, send me the details.'

The customer would actually appreciate using direct debit but had not thought about it as a need when making the telephone call. It was, therefore, a latent need.

To achieve these interactions, the call centre agent needs to create rapport and then listen carefully so as to think about what other products or services the customer really would appreciate. The agent then needs to make the suggestion in a way that makes it sound attractive. The process must seem natural. People are astute and do not want to be force-fed a product down the telephone. They can also be sensitive, so that even if they do have a latent need for a service they will still resent any hard sell when they rang about something completely different. However, many people are receptive to these kinds of approach as long as they are handled well.

Joanne Smith, manager of one of the Prudential's call centres, and Fiona Hall, now an independent coach but formerly a coach in Smith's team, are firmly convinced that coaching is the best way of ensuring that staff work to the required high standards. Hall says that telling call centre agents how to solve common problems or handle situations rarely worked. For example, she recalls telling agents that they are supposed to give their name at the beginning of the conversation and that they should put a Post-It® note on their screens to remind themselves. Nobody did this, and the agents continually forgot to give their name. Hall then realised that by using coaching skills the desired result was achieved: she was able to uncover what the learner thought would work for them, rather than what she thought would work for them. For example, some agents gave their name at a different point in the conversation. Others used visualisation techniques to help them remember, imagining shaking hands with the customer in their heads, and some agents preferred to put a marker on their screens.

Sean Moran, who was formerly a senior manager in a call centre, believes it is important not to be prescriptive with staff. He is against scripting conversations for the agents. He does, however, believe that you need to set general guidance – for instance, emphasising to staff the importance of introducing themselves by giving their name and saying 'How can I help?'

The general guidance needs to include behavioural indicators. To produce these behavioural indicators, Julia Blandford has used a proprietary customer satisfaction framework, which sets out quality indicators.

She has then fleshed these out, identifying desirable behaviours or outcomes that would be more likely to be demonstrated under each of them. She developed these behavioural indicators by listening to tapes of call centre agents and identifying the approaches that worked best. Having a framework such as this gives the coaching structure and enables the coach to focus on strengths as well as areas to improve. It also gives a strong message about where the business is going, for instance, by emphasising the importance of cross-selling and adding value to the customer's experience.

Smith and Hall also used a model of customer satisfaction at the Prudential; in their case it is a '5-star' model. They developed this rating system by asking their customers what they wanted from the call centre and built the sheet around these expectations. They also fleshed out the behavioural indicators, but they did so by obtaining input from their customers, whereas Blandford's approach has been to analyse and identify best practice from their existing call centre agents.

I believe both ways of developing standards to be equally valid, and the choice will depend on circumstances. It is also important to obtain input from staff. This can be done at the outset when drawing up the indicators, during the training, or by setting up a trial period and seeking employees' input at the end of this period.

What are the advantages and disadvantages of rating systems?

A rating system such as the one used by Smith and Hall has advantages and disadvantages. It helps establish consistency of practice and also gives a framework for and a focus to the coaching and the quest for performance improvement. The disadvantages are from the learner's point of

CASE STUDY continued

view. It can create a rigid marking structure and it also relies on the coaches' interpretations. These are not always consistent. Perhaps more critically, with some calls it is impossible to achieve the highest ranking because of the nature of the call or the conduct of the caller. This causes frustration. The coaches try to overcome this by using a mix of calls in each coaching session. The Prudential also allowed the coaches to use their own discretion and give a '5-star' rating if the agent had done everything possible. An agent can also ask for another coach to re-rate the call for extra validity.

How can consistency be achieved?

It is important for the coaches to be clear about the quality standards that need to be achieved. Smith and Hall have done this by analysing the quality ratings assigned in the coaching sessions. They also made sure coaches met together once a month to listen to a range of calls and discuss where they gave differing ratings. This helped achieve consistency and was also a valuable learning session.

How can an organisation get coaching started and accepted?

The organisations I have spoken to all say that coaching is key to enabling the call centre staff to achieve the desired standards of service and continuously develop their skills.

However, to get newly recruited staff started, training is the most effective technique. The employees working for Smith attended a six-week training programme in which they learned both the technical and the behavioural side of their jobs.

Moran believes that initial training for call centre staff must include communication skills, looking at the way the agents speak, the energy they put into the conversation, how they sit and how they control the conversation.

The coaching sessions

One-to-one coaching then starts, in the first instance, as a follow-on to the training but then continues as a means of helping people achieve the desired service levels. Just as importantly, it makes them feel valued and can help them with their development. Being a call centre agent can be a lonely job, and so feedback and empathy such as through one-to-one coaching sessions are really important.

Coaching can also help with performance improvement. Hall describes some common situations: 'I've coached many consultants whose call duration has been longer than average. We first look at why this is and then tackle it. For example, it might be that an agent is being "kept on the line" by talkative callers and they need to discover tactful ways of cutting the conversations short. Or maybe their calls are too long because of their typing speed.'

Initially, sessions are run once a week, but as the agent gains experience this can be reduced to once or twice a month.

There are two particularly critical tools required for call centre coaching. One is the tape-recording of conversations and the other is having some kind of framework against which to assess the level of service provided.

Blandford, Moran, Smith and Hall all cite the value of getting people to listen to themselves on tape. Coach and learner can work through the tapes together. The learner can 'self-critique' and self-coach, and the coach is then able to work with the learner to explore solutions and identify the things done well to build up confidence. 'Self-observation, if managed effectively and sold in the right way, is a fantastic development tool and encourages the individual to take ownership' (Hall).

Blandford and Hall have both found that many people are initially against the idea of tape-recordings and hate hearing their own voices played back to them, but they generally get used to it and then appreciate its value.

Hall finds that most people appreciate the coaching but some are anxious to get the session over with quickly. This is usually because they are either shy about having so much attention focused on them or worried about being caught out.

Setting the coaching goals

In her coaching sessions, Hall says:

The tone of the sessions is very much 'How are things going?', 'What are your training needs and concerns?'

We start with some fact-finding and do this by playing, usually, five calls for each session. We stop after each, and I discuss with the consultant what they liked and what they didn't like and what they should do differently. Then we agree the 5-star rating.

I always talk them through the good points and, as far as possible, get them to identify three or four points to work on. At first, you do not get a lot back from the consultants because they don't know and are not able to come up with the solution, so you need to point them in the right direction. This changes as they gain experience.

Hall finds a ratings system very helpful for focusing the coaching conversation. At each coaching session, the coach makes notes on how the learner performs against each of the identified standards. The aim is to achieve an 'outstanding' rating. If you achieve a middle rating, this is fine but the customer is more likely to go elsewhere, so coach and learner need to explore how to handle such an interaction so the agent can achieve an outstanding rating.

How can the coaching be sure to link into the bigger picture?

As with all business processes, a customer service ethos needs to be linked into the bigger organisational picture.

CASE STUDY continued

At one of the UK's leading credit card companies, for example, when it focused on developing a strong customer service ethos, which it underpinned through coaching, it integrated the new way of doing things with its overall objectives.

The company identified values and objectives for each of 'company, customer and colleagues'. This placed customer service and the coaching programme in context. It showed that coaching would not be something that was just nice to have but a critical tool for achieving corporate objectives.

The company also introduced a new performance appraisal programme based on the output required and the behaviours perceived as important. It conducted an annual survey of all staff, looking at cultural improvements, recognising the value added to the organisation, and identifying issues that needed addressing.

The coaching will only work in a receptive culture. One of the high-street banks, for example, found that coaching would not work in its own existing culture. It was a fast-paced environment but service quality was poor, the systems were not in place and induction training had a 'sheep-dip' mentality about it. In this kind of environment, the systems were not in place to underpin the coaching, and the management style was inappropriate. For coaching to work, it is important that managers embody the behaviours that the coaching is intended to impart; otherwise coaching is seen simply as a way of finding fault.

In successful call centres, where coaching is critical to maintaining standards, the wider corporate culture is generally one that believes people make a difference to the customer and therefore to business success. There tends to be greater empowerment and freedom to act, with people thinking outside the confines of procedures. As Blandford puts it, what is needed is a 'What can we do to help the customer?' attitude rather than 'We cannot do that because of what it says in the books.'

As we have already seen in this book, to be successful a coaching culture needs a supportive management style from the top. Blandford cites Moran who, as the senior manager in one of the call centres where she had worked, had a highly participative style of management and was only directive when it was absolutely necessary. Blandford believes that coaching can only work effectively where managers use a participative style and where they are completely on board with the customer service ethos and the role of coaching. She has found many managers were uncomfortable with this, believing they need to show they are 'experts' and prove their worth by giving people the answers. It is important to work with them to enable them to change their style and become enablers who trust people to come up with their own solutions. This is an important observation for HR professionals who wish to introduce coaching into a command-and-control environment.

Blandford finds also that it is important to embed a language in the culture to help people articulate quality service. Many managers just listen to a call and then say, 'Oh, that was a good call', or 'You sounded friendly.' She has had to work extensively with them to get them to identify the behaviours that make a call good. 'It was a steady pace, you sounded confident', or 'The pace was quick – you sounded less certain' or, 'Sometimes, I notice, when you answer a question, your pitch goes up at the end and it sounds like another question. If you can bring the pitch down, it will work better. We can play this back on tape.' Blandford believes it is essential for all managers to use the same language as the coaches and the call centre agents so that they can give feedback to staff and set development goals with them.

How is performance measured in a call centre?

As in all areas of business, measurement is essential, but it also needs to be wisely identified and wisely used, as it can both create tensions and distort behaviour in unintended ways.

Most call centre agents have sales targets, targets to generate referrals or to sell some particular product, which can lead to some people being too focused at selling these things. It is a fine balance between effective selling and ensuring the customer only receives a product that meets their needs. That is another area where coaching can be very effective: coaches sometimes need to keep agents in check to ensure they are not overselling a particular product.

Measuring the effectiveness of the coaching

Most call centres track all sorts of different things. Productivity, as in the number of calls taken, and other quantitative measures are easy to identify but used alone can cause problems. For this reason, many call centres also use qualitative measures such as customer satisfaction surveys, staff perception surveys and overall scores from the rating scales.

Moran believes the balance between quality and productivity is a delicate one, but that if you get the quality right, the productivity comes along. He believes also there is a pull between answering customer calls and taking people off for coaching. For coaching to work there has to be the right staffing levels. You have to do a cost-benefit analysis and you need to identify the cost of not doing it. If you do not coach, there is a potentially enormous cost arising from errors and lower customer satisfaction. Customers prefer to wait longer and get better service. Accountants like the calls answered quickly. Also you need to weigh up what is important for different topics. Words and numbers tell different stories. For example, in some call centres a target to prove the value of coaching might be that the number of calls is reduced. Using the example given earlier, if someone can be persuaded to switch to direct debit, they will no longer call in every month to check the payment has gone through. The reduction in the number of calls may outweigh the increase in time taken over each call and lead to cost savings.

As with all measures, there are often other factors that need to be taken into account. For example, some call centres are in areas where there is a high or low staff turnover: high staff turnover will inevitably lead to lower productivity and lower customer satisfaction, but this does not necessarily mean that coaching is less effective just because the results of that particular centre are poor. On the contrary, results might have been far worse without an effective coaching programme.

Smith is convinced the value of coaching is proven. Before coaching was introduced to her team, staff were constantly taking moans and gripes to the staff representative committee. Once the coaching was underway, this changed and it was clear that people felt 'empowered to make a difference; they are not told what to do and they have the opportunity to input into the way things are done and what goes on'. Smith has also found that 'coaching results in fewer mistakes, better use of systems, sharing of best practice within the team, people pick up more tips, quality control is better, and the coaching creates opportunities for new business. It also makes people feel valued and they are more likely to strive to improve. The business benefits by achieving better customer service and higher productivity.'

Measuring the individual coach

Measuring the effectiveness of the coach is important but problematic. In one call centre, the team manager observed the coach in action, using a series of pointers. People were self-conscious about this at first but gradually accepted the idea. This does, however, create the problem of destroying the confidentiality that is so essential to the relationship between coach and learner. That is partly overcome by the fact that observations only relate to a minority of coaching sessions, and the learner is forewarned. Some companies video coaching sessions, though this can create similar problems. Some coaches do their own surveys: 'I want to improve what I do for you. How can I do it better?' Some ask for feedback at the end of the session, but this is less successful as the learner needs time to reflect. In most call centres, coaches are measured through a mixture of surveys, anecdotal evidence and statistics.

Blandford feels that where senior managers take a more active interest, the coaches perform better and keep better documentation. From their experience, Smith and Hall both believe there is still an emphasis on the technical and that first and foremost the coach is judged on results. 'Have you shown you keep new entrants, that they stay longer and are more motivated and are therefore saving money on attrition?' These assessments come through colleague feedback and from the overall measures used for the call centre.

Team coach or manager coach

Who carries out the coaching is a question with which all the call centres in my analysis have grappled. Should it be the manager/team leader? The manager/team leader is after all responsible for the results achieved by the call centre agents. Or should there be dedicated coaches whose only responsibility is the coaching? If there are dedicated coaches, should the coaches work as part of the team, reporting to the manager/team leader, or should there be a separate team of coaches? What are the implications of either arrangement? Does this create tensions? How can these tensions be overcome?

The benefits of having dedicated, non-managerial coaches who make up a separate team are that you get tighter control around consistency. At one call centre I analysed there are 100 in the centre with five on the coaching team. It is easy for them to stop listening to tapes individually and listen to the same call together and come to a consensus. Having dedicated coaches brings the added advantages that it is the whole purpose of their job and they do not get interrupted by other responsibilities. Perhaps the most compelling reason is that they are not also responsible for performance and so the coach can speak freely with them.

The downside of having dedicated coaches is that the manager does not hear their staff directly and regularly, and this weakens their ability to input into the person's development. In such circumstances, they are reliant on quality monitoring to provide them with the information they need to manage effectively. Manager and coach also need to be able to forge a relationship that provides the manager with what they need to know to enable them to manage effectively and ensure targets are met, while protecting the necessary confidentiality between coach and learner.

However, some call centres have found that coaches sometimes get bored listening to calls all the time and have sought ways of dealing with this. Coaches can be given an overall remit to improve the quality and quantity of calls. This then naturally involves them in additional projects and responsibilities, such as keeping up-to-date on changes in legislation and regulations and data protection, developing special training courses, or facilitating away-days. A different solution is being tried by one financial services organisation, which is setting up a coaching pool that people will rotate in and out of.

Relationship between coaching and reward

Some call centres have a quality assurance team that analyses the performance scores that feed into the annual review and influence the agent's end-of-year rating and bonus allocation. There is a downside to this, as people associate the coaching too closely with the bonus and fight tooth and nail over their ratings. This then makes the ratings a barrier to development, thus defeating their primary purpose. Either coaching needs to be seen as helpful to ensuring continually improving ratings or a wider set of measures needs to be established for bonus and salary review purposes.

Managing a call centre is notoriously difficult. Their growth has given rise to a whole series of challenging personnel management issues, and coaching features prominently among the solutions for these.

KEY LEARNING POINTS
Comparing and contrasting coaching at BBC Newsgathering and in call centres

In both situations coaching is a highly effective way of achieving high standards of performance and keeping ahead of the competition. At BBC Newsgathering, the coaching is also about maximising the potential of new technology.

Both examples illustrate the effectiveness of coaching as a tool for enabling people to develop and strive for continuous improvement. In BBC Newsgathering, it is also about keeping up with a very rapid pace of change.

In both situations, we see the importance of having clearly identified performance standards against which to pitch the coaching. We see the necessity of the skills coaches being well respected for their experience and expertise. We also see the importance of enabling the learner to self-critique.

Both examples illustrate the importance of integrating the coaching and what it sets out to achieve with other processes. They also clearly show how crucial it is for the coaches to have a continuous dialogue with the management and with the other functions of the business with which their learners interact, so that the coaching is not carried out in isolation.

The BBC as a whole has a very clear purpose, as does the Newsgathering team. The effect of these guiding principles is to allow maximum scope for individuality, creativity and innovation. In such a fluid, fast-moving set-up, it is essential for the coaches to keep up-to-date with what is going on both within and outside the organisation.

In the call centre environment, the work and the way it is performed is very much more pre-scribed, and the coaching is a way of giving individuals control over how they carry out their tasks and responsibilities. In this kind of environment, it is important to think through how coaching is to be used, what it is to achieve and how it integrates with other people processes such as remuneration, reward and performance management. The relationship between coach and line manager and the place of the coach within the departmental set-up also need to be carefully thought through.

Both case studies show that coaching programmes work best where the leadership style is collaborative, rather than command and control. Command-and-control managers can be helped to take on the new behaviours through training, coaching, focused development initiatives and appropriate reward and recognition.

CASE STUDY 3

Coaching in a high-tech business

High-tech businesses and IT departments, whether entrepreneurial start-ups or well-established, are exciting and energising places to work. Typically, people who work in these environments are highly skilled, task-oriented individuals who are motivated and stimulated by their work and anxious to keep up with the fast pace of change in their field.

People often work on discrete tasks, perhaps pursuing their own line of discovery, and it becomes difficult to keep sight of the larger project and stay in touch with what others are doing. There is often an over-reliance on e-mail communication and insufficient face-to-face contact. People frequently work on flexible teams and may have little day-to-day contact with their line managers. Tensions often arise when people required to maintain existing technology feel aggrieved that they are not assigned to the latest, cutting-edge developments, even though their expertise might be highly valued and needed.

What are the business reasons for introducing coaching?

Coaching, especially among peers, can help solve some of these problems. Steve Roche, now an independent coach, provides an example from a situation he faced when working in an IT department. He needed to overcome resistance to a new way of working. By adopting a coaching style rather than using a directive approach, Roche found that people far more readily committed to change. Roche listened to them, acknowledged their achievements and encouraged them to identify how things should be done: 'What are your interests?' 'What helps you do well?' 'What is your big issue today?' 'What is stopping you being really effective?' As a result, Roche and his colleagues created a more exciting environment where people worked on short, sharp projects, in contrast to the old way of having projects grinding on for months. This benefited the end user, as well as the development team.

BTexact Technologies, BT's advanced communication technologies business, is an example of an organisation that uses coaching to get the best from its employees. BTexact helps businesses and organisations gain maximum advantage from communications technology. It employs around 2,700 technologists, including some who are world experts in their specialist fields.

To encourage its people to think more about how they work and interact with their colleagues, BTexact's human resources team ran a competition asking people to submit ideas on what coaching meant to them. Anita Traynor, People Manager, eBusiness Services, won the competition and received, in addition to a personal prize, £500 to be spent on personal development or on developing a coaching network. Traynor decided to do the latter.

Implementing the coaching

The network, which is now thriving, proved popular right from the start. The monthly lunchtime events provide people with a taster of something that is quite different from their usual day-to-day activities. They gain new ideas and a broader perspective on work and managing relationships. Traynor describes the network events as being 'akin to having some space and a haven to do something creative and different'. Many people network and coach one another between events. Traynor is now seeking funding so that they can engage higher-profile speakers for the events. She aims for an attendance of around 20 at the meetings. Although anyone can come along to an event, the network advertises initially to a closed mailing list, as the intention is to keep each event small enough for participants to interact. Traynor also uses the mailing list to match mentors and learners.

Most of the people who attend the events are technical staff. Some are part of teams but many work alone. The network helps to make the working day more interesting, lively and enjoyable by adding both a social dimension and a different intellectual stimulus. The events give people a taster of different ways of doing things which they can then try out later. For example, after sessions on managing meetings and making presentations, most people tried out the ideas.

Traynor strongly supports the view that there are particular benefits to using a coaching style in a technical environment. It helps people feel valued as individuals and not just used as a robot resource. Coaching helps people to understand and develop their interpersonal skills. It is the best way to work with individual line managers and helps people get the best from their careers.

There are so many different, complex projects going on in the business that they can seem like many independent activities. When people move from one project to another, it can be a struggle for them to get into the new project. The processes that can help them know how to get things done are on the company's intranet. Coaching can support the other part – the social aspect of getting to know people, getting and sharing information, and so on.

If someone moves project, they will be assigned to a colleague who can show them the ropes. Graduates are always assigned a buddy. Traynor cites the example of one person finding it difficult to get to grips with a new project. He had had two days off with a stress-related illness, had been very miserable and went to ask for help. He was assigned a coach, one of the people from the network, and then progressed in leaps and bounds. This person was not naturally outgoing and tended to see only the technical issues. The coach helped him identify the 'social' issues he needed to think about and also to point him in the right direction in terms of who he needed to speak to, and so on. His attitude and performance both improved as a result of the coaching.

Traynor also cites other examples where coaching has helped people getting into projects much more quickly than used to be the case. There is no formal training in coaching skills, but the skills and content of coaching, goal-setting, personal visioning and values are all covered in the network events.

How does the coaching fit into the culture and processes of the organisation?

The management culture at BTexact Technologies positively encourages coaching. Formal coaching is arranged for many people, where this is appropriate. Most of the top managers have coaches, as do people who are promoted to positions where they manage others. Mentoring is common in the organisation but is not formally organised.

Organising the network events and matching mentors and learners takes Traynor around 2–3 days a month. She performs most of the tasks in her own time and in addition to doing a full week's work. BTexact Technologies has a flexible-working environment, which helps Traynor arrange her time effectively. All staff are able to arrange their own working time: the focus is on getting the job done. Traynor's contract does not include a specified working day but is based around the job specification. She also enjoys the advantage of roving technology and remote Internet access enabling her to work in the office, from home or elsewhere.

What are the skills and techniques required for 'peer coaching'?

All coaching requires strong interpersonal skills, especially building rapport, listening and questioning. These are examined in Chapter 10. Peer coaching, as with coaching performed in a managerial role, is more likely to be given in spontaneous circumstances, rather than as a tailored programme. The 'SNIP' model and the other pointers offered in Chapter 2 apply equally well to peer coaching.

KEY LEARNING POINTS

Peer coaching is an effective way of getting people to share knowledge and expertise and can be exceptionally useful for project teams, especially where people work on discrete tasks within the whole project. It is also a successful means for gaining acceptance to change, as it encourages people to recognise the need for change and be involved in the design of the new system.

The coaching network at BTexact Technologies is an example of how coaching can add a people dimension to otherwise completely task-oriented work and how it can help give people a broader perspective and a wider range of skill sets. The network itself is an immensely interesting initiative and one that other organisations could consider encouraging.

The human resources team at BTexact Technologies focused on enabling and facilitating people policies, as opposed to policing and implementation. To operate in this way requires greater skills of visioning, innovation and influencing.

Coaching in the arts industry

Coaching and mentoring have played a critical role in the arts industry for many years. There is a great deal of informal mentoring probably because, by its nature, this is an environment where interpersonal relationships are important and where people traditionally learn by observing and copying.

The arts industry has a strong public service ethos, with many organisations operating on a not-for-profit basis. Undoubtedly, as a result, there is more informal and voluntary mentoring, and everyone is more inclined to volunteer to take on unpaid roles. Most people feel that they get powerful emotional rewards working in the arts, and this too makes them feel they want to give something back.

The term 'mentoring' is more commonly used in this sector than 'coaching'. In the introduction to this book, I stated that I use the terms 'coaching' and 'mentoring' almost interchangeably, and that I would use 'coaching' as the composite term. The main reason I regard the terms as interchangeable is that I believe that mentors almost always need to coach people as part of the mentoring relationship. I think, therefore, that it is helpful if mentors also see themselves as coaches.

Nonetheless, I believe there often are differences between coaching and mentoring and that it can sometimes be helpful to draw distinctions between the two. For example, a mentor is usually more experienced and qualified than the learner. The relationship fostered with the learner is often one of being a trusted adviser, and they may provide support to the learner over an extended period of time. A coach enables, has a shorter and sometimes time-bound relationship, and focuses more on immediate results.

In the following examples (and bearing in mind the Witherspoon coaching continuum – Chapter 3), I keep to the term used by the people and organisations featured. Whatever the terminology, I believe that these initiatives add to our understanding of the value of coaching as a strategic solution.

What are the business reasons for introducing coaching?

In the early 1980s, Jodi Myers, then working at the UK Arts Council as marketing officer for the national touring programme, was faced with a shortage of people in arts marketing, especially at post-entry level. One of the causes of this shortage was a lack of formal career structure. To overcome this problem, Myers established a scheme offering bursaries for young people to undertake an 'apprenticeship' with an established arts organisation. As part of this scheme, a mentor was appointed for each trainee. The mentor was someone outside the trainee's own organisation who could act as a sounding board and adviser to the trainee during the 'apprenticeship'.

The scheme ran for a number of years very successfully, and many apprentices went on to become senior marketing people at various prestigious arts organisations and events such as the Edinburgh Festival.

Is this typical or are the arts, then, any different from other parts of the private and public sectors? Debbie Kingsley, who as part of her job acts as a coach and mentor to people in the arts, believes that the sector is much less well-organised than other sectors at arranging formal development programmes and training courses. Largely this is because arts organisations cannot easily afford these programmes, and relatively low pay means that individuals cannot easily finance their own studies. As a result people have to find other ways to develop their careers and gain certain skills.

Since the first exercise introduced by the Arts Council, both formal and informal mentoring and coaching have become commonplace in the arts industry, which has also become extremely adept at making mentoring arrangements.

Myers believes that mentoring schemes offer opportunities to young people to meet experienced people and seek assistance that are simply not available to them in the normal working environment. Mentoring is also particularly valuable as a person progresses in their career and moves away from their initial area of technical competence, taking on broader challenges and responsibilities.

Many learners previously granted bursaries for mentoring were high-potential people on a fast track for development. They were usually attached to leading arts organisations such as the Royal Shakespeare Company, Welsh National Opera or regional arts organisations, where there were exciting opportunities. At that time, the learners' employing organisations would neither have had the funds nor the administrative experience to organise training and mentoring schemes of this kind.

Implementing the coaching

One of the earliest lessons learned about mentoring in the arts industry is that even the most brilliant and talented natural marketers, who seem to have good coaching styles, do not always make good mentors. Organisations across all sectors have had similar experiences and have found that mentors benefit from some formal preparation for the role. Ideally, this preparation takes the form of formal, structured training, covering the ins and outs of mentoring and giving some theoretical underpinning. An example is given in the case study below on the Arts Marketing Association. It is generally found that where mentors are appropriately prepared for the role, both parties find the mentoring sessions became more focused and productive.

At the Arts Council it was also discovered that a great deal of confusion and administrative effort were saved by having clear contractual arrangements and a well-defined process for appointing mentors and learners, and for managing the relationship. As part of this process Myers believes it is important to include the learner in the selection process: she always made a point of reviewing the background of the proposed mentor with the learner before the appointment was finalised. As well as helping ensure compatibility between mentor and learner, having clear contractual arrangements also ensures both parties have a good idea of what they are committing themselves to, as regards the nature of the relationship, the time and effort it will require, confidentiality and how progress will be monitored and measured.

In another, more recent, mentoring initiative, the executives of London Arts (an arts funding and development organisation) were eager to diversify their workforce. They had set up trainee officer posts, aimed at helping people from minority groups move up the career path. These posts included mentoring and also a week's placement with an arts organisation.

In her current capacity as Director of Performing Arts at the Royal Festival Hall, Myers acted as mentor to someone, meeting her regularly over a period of about eight months and being available on the telephone between meetings. At the end of the initial period, Myers's learner and the others on the scheme successfully applied for advertised jobs. At the end of this mentoring period, both mentor and learner went through a debriefing with a third party who assessed the scheme.

Myers herself has regularly, and over many years, called upon people she used to work with to give her informal mentoring on work-related issues. She believes that such relationships are common in the arts industry.

Kingsley's role, in contrast, is to work as a coach and mentor, on a formal, paid basis, to people in the arts world. One of her roles is to mentor arts development officers for local authorities, a role

Kingsley has herself held previously. Her learners in the local authorities may have a great deal of experience in the arts but be in their first local authority posting.

Kingsley also finds that she is sometimes asked to fix up mentors from the commercial world for senior arts people. This enables the arts people to learn broader strategic skills.

Based on the experiences of her early scheme, Myers recommends that when choosing mentors, the following criteria should be applied. Mentors should:

- work in organisations that are already committed to training or, if they are self-employed, demonstrate such a commitment

- be able to give learners a broad overview

- be interested in and committed to the process

- be available both with the time and geographical proximity to meet the learner.

Myers also places a lot of store on confidentiality. She believes that sometimes you go to a mentor to discuss sensitive personal issues that you would not share with your internal personnel department.

CASE STUDY 5

The Arts Marketing Association

The Arts Marketing Association is a professional development body for those with an interest in the relationship between people and the arts. It has 1,350 members in the UK from across the arts sector.

One of the services the Arts Marketing Association provides is a learner-driven mentoring scheme, in its third year in 2003. Applications are received from mentors and learners and are grouped into cohorts. When they have sufficient numbers for a cohort, learners and mentors attend a training day, for which there is a nominal £25 charge, and then people are paired up. Some 150 learners on the scheme had entered at the time of writing.

Qualification requires being a member of the Association to train, and at least five years' professional experience in the sector to be a mentor. The training day covers such subjects as: What is the mentoring process? How does it work and why? What skills would a receptive learner have? What skills would an effective mentor have? It also includes a programme of exercises to enable delegates to understand, practise and develop the skills.

At the end of the day, delegates set out their objectives and practical constraints (such as availability and location). Kate Fortescue of the Arts Marketing Association works with the mentors to identify their strengths and then identifies suitable learners. She contacts the learner to discuss the prospective mentor, and she then goes to the mentor and finally back to the learner, who makes the contact. Learners and mentors may have already met on the training day, or know each other from elsewhere, but this is not always the case. The learner is in complete control of the choice of mentor, with Fortescue advising.

The process moves forward with Fortescue getting participants to articulate what they want to get out of the relationship and seeing to the contractual details: the length of the sessions, the frequency of the meetings and the length of the project. This will typically be between 18 and 24 months. If it continues beyond 24 months the association no longer keeps records, because it is believed the relationship will have matured, and the parties are then colleagues getting together for a chat. Goals are also reviewed at 6 and 12 months.

The Arts Marketing Association set up the scheme because research showed a very high demand from its membership, many of whom expressed a sense of isolation. This results from the fact that in some organisations there is only one person responsible for marketing. Also it was found that many people were frustrated because there was a feeling that the wheel was constantly being reinvented: their experience in the field of Arts Marketing was not being passed on to newcomers.

From the formal and informal monitoring that the Arts Marketing Association carries out of the scheme, it has also found that the mentors themselves learn and develop considerably through the experience.

The Arts Marketing Association gives line managers information about the benefits of the scheme. Most line managers support their learners and are usually pleased for them to participate, perhaps because this relieves them of some pressure. There have, however, been some difficulties with line managers. Some learners felt unable to tell their line manager they were being mentored. Some line managers wanted the right of veto over the mentor.

The Arts Marketing Association seeks to resolve such conflicts, working through, with the learner, why they feel they cannot be open with their line manager. They address such issues as how much of this awkwardness is coming from the line manager and how much from the learner, and discuss whether mentoring is a public or private relationship. In the end, this is a facilitative scheme, driven by the learner, and the decision to inform their line manager is up to them. They are, however, encouraged to do so.

Pam Henderson, the Director of the Arts Marketing Association, also supports the view expressed above that the mentoring scheme benefits from a great sense of altruism and openness in the arts. No one on the Arts Marketing Association scheme gets paid for being a mentor, and some people meet outside of work. The Arts Marketing Association events are all about participants sharing; they are extremely open about the audiences they receive and their marketing practices. Visiting speakers from outside the arts are often shocked at what they are being asked to reveal. Those from the commercial world have a much greater sense of confidentiality and sensitivity of information, and of not discussing things that went wrong. The commercial world is also less receptive to the idea of training someone so that they are able to take on a larger post in another organisation.

From the feedback received it is clear that many learners felt their mentors opened doors for them that enabled them to get another job. They believe the new knowledge and skills gained have helped them to resolve problems that seemed insurmountable. The scheme has retained mentors and most relationships last. Henderson believes this bears testimony to the success of the scheme. Only three pairings came to an end and, of these, one was because one of the pair moved away. One relationship did not work, and she believes this was because it was a bad pairing.

As Kingsley puts it, 'Most people working in the arts believe that there is a whole world of interesting people out there and that it is important to ask constantly, "Who can I learn from?"'

KEY LEARNING POINTS

Coaching in the arts industry is a strategic solution for the sector as a whole. It aims to help overcome skills shortages, spread good practices and ideas, develop people and create development paths. It has also been used to create a more diverse workforce, and is a good example of performance coaching in action

Formally training coaches, mentors and learners in preparation for taking up their roles is immensely beneficial. The training may cover the interpersonal skills, such as listening and questioning, or the process, such as how to structure the sessions, set goals and so on.

Contractual arrangements help set expectations and clarify matters such as timing and frequency of the meetings, confidentiality, reviews, and so on.

Relationships work best when the learner controls the choice of coach (mentor), as this increases the likelihood of the two people being compatible. It also makes both parties feel more confident about the relationship.

A third party has a distinct and valuable role to play in setting up and monitoring coaching arrangements. They can advise on the pairing of coach and learner; make contractual arrangements; provide training on the skills and the process; be available to provide any impartial advice required; and monitor and review arrangements to ensure the coaching achieves the desired results.

The use of a (paid) coach (or mentor) for the 'lone' person who is the only specialist in the organisation is also interesting. It is always difficult for the person who has no fellow professionals in the organisation to help them learn, develop and innovate. There are many HR people who find themselves in similar circumstances. Using a coach compensates for these difficulties and is also a way of bringing in professional ideas from the outside. This is a solution that could usefully be taken up by HR people working in small organisations. Heads of small businesses also stand to gain from an outside coach (or mentor).

5
Career development coaching

Coaching people for career development is one of the most common forms of coaching offered by organisations. As we saw in an earlier chapter, professional service firms, and other organisations that tend towards flat hierarchies, offer career development coaching to people to help ensure everyone has an even chance of being considered for partnership or to be appointed as directors. In these cases, career coaching is usually available following participation at a career development centre. Many organisations run career development coaching for graduate trainees, or for people on their fast-track programme or who are undergoing assessment for entry to a fast-track programme.

Lloyds TSB runs a career development coaching programme that is available to all staff. The aim of its programme has been to reduce turnover by making people aware of the opportunities open to them within the organisation.

Why should an organisation introduce career development coaching? How should this be set up? What infrastructure is required? How does it work? How are the coaches selected? How is success measured? Are there conflicts with line managers? How does coaching fit in with other processes? How do you train the career coaches? How do you manage the career coaches and their activities?

In this chapter, I will address these questions by focusing specifically on the example of Lloyds TSB.

CASE STUDY

Career coaching at Lloyds TSB

What were the business reasons for introducing career coaching?

Lloyds TSB has focused over the last few years on career management. In the 1980s, people's careers had been managed for them by their manager, but during the 1990s there was a sea change: the business restructured continuously, matrix structures became commonplace and people were encouraged to take responsibility for their own careers.

Staff employee surveys were showing that employees did not have sufficient information to enable them to manage their careers. They found that people felt uneasy when using the word 'career'.

Staff also felt they had no help in managing career opportunities. Perception often differs from reality, and according to Rob Briggs, who is responsible for the career development programme, this was certainly the case at Lloyds TSB. In spite of this perception, there had been a record number of internal promotions over several years.

What is the infrastructure?

It was against this background that Lloyds TSB management decided to set up a Centre for Career Management. This is the company's international career centre for giving information, advice, guidance and coaching to help people manage their careers.

The centre has a dedicated site on the intranet and initial contact is through the HR call centre where all employees can contact a team of learning and development advisers. These advisers identify and discuss individual needs, give advice and, if required, put people in touch with a fully trained career coach. The learning and development advisers action a high percentage of the calls received, providing staff with easy access to high-quality advice and guidance

There are over a hundred career coaches handling cases in addition to their normal jobs. To become a career coach, individuals follow an extensive training programme leading to assessment and recognition by the Institute of Career Guidance. The coaches' role is to work with the people and through coaching help them develop their career plan.

How does the career coaching work?

The HR Call Centre is able to handle much of the information people require about different career options and job opportunities. Those who require further help are put in touch with a career coach.

The career coaches support individuals in the development of their career plans. They hold an exploratory meeting and a follow-up career discussion. This may challenge people on issues such as their objectives, how they will achieve them and how they have drawn up their CVs.

Coaches aim to build confidence and provide support. The coaches have also been trained in diversity issues and have information at their disposal about the different job possibilities within the organisation so that they can give impartial, unbiased advice. This impartiality and 'breadth' makes the service quite different in nature and separate from any career advice that line managers may give.

Career coaches also carry out follow-up sessions with people in which they may discuss 'blockages' that are preventing the individual from achieving his or her aims. Having a mentor may be one of the actions identified and Lloyds TSB run an extensive mentoring database, which is also available to all staff.

The career development service is used by staff at all levels in the organisation. It is not seen as something to do only in a crisis but as a proactive way to manage your career and, as a result, take-up is high.

How are the career coaches selected?

At first, career coaches were selected from Lloyds TSB's population of training staff, because they were already experienced facilitators, and many were also experienced coaches with good coaching skills.

Following the initial success of the service the possibility of being trained as a career coach was offered more broadly to all HR people. Senior HR managers were originally trained to coach senior people but, in fact, Lloyds TSB finds that it is not a problem to have a person with a relatively junior role in the organisation coach senior staff and vice versa.

The group is now looking at training 50 line managers who have completed an assessment to join a senior management development programme to become career coaches. This could have a significant impact on the future of the business, as it will create a pool of future leaders who are committed to people development and coaching.

The response from line managers to the request for volunteers has been huge because they feel that the company has given them an opportunity to develop themselves; also acting as career coaches enables them to 'give something back' to their work community.

From the start, the scheme had the active backing of the Group HR Business Director, who was one of the first to be trained as a coach and who ensured all his team members were also trained. This support is seen as significant in helping to raise the profile of the scheme.

How is success measured?

Lloyds TSB decided to seek accreditation for its scheme with the Department for Education and Skills and they were first to achieve the Matrix Quality Standard through the Guidance Accreditation Board.

The main benefit of the accreditation is that it shows that the scheme operates to certain standards, especially those that guarantee confidentiality.

Some career coaching is linked to development and diversity programmes. These links are important as they add value to the coaching and show that it is proactive and not just for a crisis.

Lloyds TSB has measured the success of the career development coaching by tracking attitudes through its employee opinion survey and by looking at staff turnover. The results of recent staff surveys show that the coaching has had a positive impact on staff attitudes and levels of satisfaction.

Are there conflicts with line managers?

Confidentiality between coach and learner is vital. If a line manager enquires about the content or results of the coaching that his staff receive he is not told but, on the other hand, staff are encouraged to talk to their line manager about their discussions.

CASE STUDY continued

There is a growing understanding that line managers need to be good people managers and good coaches. When the scheme was first launched, many line managers called on behalf of their staff. It is also significant that many line managers have been through selection and assessment centres, which has raised awareness of the importance of people development.

There have been no complaints from line managers about their staff receiving the coaching or about their staff being involved as coaches, and Lloyds TSB is even finding that many people are voluntarily coming in for coaching during their time off.

How does the career coaching fit in with other processes?

The company's intranet website is the focal point for information and access to learning, and there are learning maps for most roles in the organisation. In the first instance, people are expected to assess themselves using online diagnostics, learning styles inventories and personality profiles. They are also expected to search for all the information that is available about particular jobs. People will therefore have completed considerable groundwork before their career coaching session. This means the coach can then discuss with them the outputs and steps for the future. The fact that so much information is readily available and that people can also do some diagnostic work before starting the coaching means that the coaches are able to achieve more in each session.

After the coaching, people are encouraged to complete the development of an action plan as a further way of encouraging action following the formal coaching session. Career coaching gives people the tools to control and take ownership of their careers and also helps people to think 'outside the box', perhaps considering vacancies that they might not previously have thought about.

All jobs are advertised internally and while previously there was a low response to internal vacancies, now people seek out and apply for the opportunities. The advantages to the organisation of internal appointments are clear: there is a saving on the costs associated with induction of new people into the organisation, and the people who are recruited become productive more quickly.

Lloyds TSB aims to make learning and development more accessible and offers programmes that use blended learning, that is, a mix of appropriate delivery media. Business pressures mean that people need easy access to learning in order to minimise time off the job and to control costs. This approach places a particular onus on people to be hungry enough for self-improvement and advancement and, to continue the metaphor, to have the appetite to follow it through. It also allows people to proceed at their own pace.

The HR call centre provides information and advice on a range of personnel and training enquiries – it averages around a thousand calls a day. Calls on training are divided into administration, career and learning advice.

As mentioned earlier, the learning and development advisers have been trained to give career development advice and can have in-depth discussions with callers to ascertain the issues and what they want to get out of the coaching. They can offer information and also send out diagnostic questionnaires. To enable them to provide this level of service, the career and learning advisers' training is similar to the career coaching training. Indeed, Lloyds TSB is now looking at the viability of carrying out career coaching by telephone.

Lloyds TSB also uses coaching for its trainers. The nature of business requirements means that training is provided around the country by teams of trainers, each of which has a team coach. The team coaches are almost always line managers and work with the trainers to review their work and their career development.

The team coaches provide coaching on training delivery. Each trainer will, on average, receive three 'observations' every half-year. Trainers view this coaching favourably and see it as a way of getting high-quality feedback that enables them to keep developing their training skills. Being a training coach can be a full-time role, although team coaches also train. The team coaches receive coaching from their line managers.

How are career coaches trained?

The training ensures all career coaches are fully equipped. The accreditation includes an external career adviser sitting with them through three career sessions.

After six months, coaches take a professional development award. To gain this award, coaches need to set objectives and complete write-ups, case notes and a reflective summary of selected cases. These are included within a portfolio, which is assessed. The coaches sometimes find it difficult to fit everything in, but the award is a beneficial benchmark and helps them know they are on the right track.

The training comprises a two- to three-day course with a one-day follow-up. To provide an effective development programme coaches with less training experience follow the longer, three-day course, which provides more training in basic facilitation skills and basic coaching first.

Making the boundaries clear is a key part of the training. First, the career coaching is only to talk about careers in Lloyds TSB. Secondly, it is about giving advice, coaching and guidance – not counselling.

The model basically addresses these issues:

- If people are unsure about the direction to take in their career, then they require coaching.

- If they are unsure of the direction they wish to take and have received coaching before, they need support from a mentor and from their line manager.

- If they have blockages in ability and are confused, then they require counselling.

Lloyds TSB finds there is sometimes a blurred line between coaching and counselling, and career coaches are trained to decide when the line is too blurred to add value. They are also trained to know when and where to go for advice. One example that is quoted was a clear stress case in which the learner broke down during a coaching session. In this instance the coach contacted the bank's medical department.

Managing the career coaches

Angie Charles is a career management consultant who worked with Rob Briggs in setting up the company's career service. She now manages the career coaches support service, which is the point of contact if they have queries or want to discuss cases. Her role includes looking at diversity issues, projects and leadership, as well as 360-degree feedback, and she also acts as the prime contact for people wanting to become coaches.

At first it was possible to get the coaches back together for discussions and networking, but because of the success of the programme there are now so many coaches that this is impractical, and they are looking at developing other networking initiatives. These include an online bulletin board for people to post and respond to particular problems or to share knowledge. A survey on how to improve the support and back-up offered to coaches has been carried out, and the feedback indicated more communication was needed.

KEY LEARNING POINTS

The following points, derived from the Lloyds TSB example, may provide good advice for other organisations considering introducing career development coaching:

- Prepare a strategic plan that identifies such issues as: 'Who will the audience be?' 'Will the coaching be exclusive or across the business?' 'How will you market this internally?'

- Having an infrastructure in place is helpful. Lloyds TSB already had a well-established and well-regarded HR call centre in place.

- Get buy-in from the top at the outset. The Group HR Business Director was enthusiastic and fully supportive. He kept people motivated, gained support from senior management and, by being trained as a coach, set a powerful example.

- Identify the benefits and talk about them widely right from the beginning. It is important to make sure the coaching is not thought of as outplacement.

- Establish guarantees of confidentiality. This helps get over initial barriers.

- Make a strong business case. This is important to show why career coaching is needed and how it will contribute to organisational success.

- Be especially careful with the selection of the first group of career coaches. They must be enthusiastic, want it to work and be prepared to take risks.

There are a number of possible pitfalls that you need to deal with in advance. You need to consider carefully the infrastructure and how the coaching will be managed. If you do not have a call centre infrastructure, you need to think carefully about how can you manage and track the career coaching.

Career coaches all have 'day jobs', and this reality has to be managed well. The career coaches should have enough cases to enable them to keep developing their expertise but not so many as to start impinging on their full-time roles.

Set up service-level agreements that clarify how frequently coaches will be required to coach, timescales, feedback etc. Be prepared for cynicism and work out some clear and consistent messages. The best way to combat cynicism is by running the programme effectively.

6

The consultant-coach

The interaction between coaching and consultancy raises two questions: first, can you success-fully be both a coach and a consultant within the same working relationship? And, secondly, to what extent do consultants need to have and apply coaching skills in the normal course of a consultancy relationship?

COACH OR CONSULTANT?

A consultant is paid to provide advice and solutions, and is held accountable for results, whereas a coach is paid for an ability to help the individual manage their own learning and identify their own solutions. These are very different, almost diametrically opposite approaches. Are they compatible? Many coaches are strict about drawing the boundary between coaching and consultancy. If they are in a coaching relationship and find the client requires consultancy advice, even if it falls within their area of expertise, they will not give it themselves but will call in an external consultant. Some coaches believe that mixing coaching with consultancy leads to highly directive coaching, which is more like teaching and does not therefore achieve the coach's prime objective of helping the individual to learn.

These are black-and-white views and there are many 'grey' instances when I would argue that it is possible – in fact, preferable – to act as both consultant and coach. Let me offer an example: I was approached by an HR manager from an American bank needing someone to work with its foreign exchange trading department. This department comprised four inexperienced man-agers, all recent appointments, who were each responsible for teams ranging from six to thirty people. The vice-president in charge was an experienced manager who placed great importance on good people management. He was keen to engage a performance coach who would work with each of his managers to develop their people management skills. However, he also wanted someone to get to know the department, the people and the managers well enough to be able to redesign their performance management processes and introduce a 360-degree feedback programme. He was therefore asking for a mix of coaching and consultancy.

We explored the possible conflict of roles. However, we decided that, in an environment that can be hostile to outsiders and addressing a series of tasks that would need to share the same knowledge and understanding of the department, it made no sense to split the coaching from the consultancy and to employ two people. In such an environment it is hard enough to get one person accepted. The potential conflict was resolved by using a coaching style, as far as possible, for the consultancy aspect of the project and by a heightened awareness of the danger of being over-directive for the coaching aspect of the assignment.

As coach to these four managers, I helped them each to develop ways of managing their departments that suited them and their styles. They developed their self-awareness of how their behaviour affected others and the environment, and gained deeper insights into what motivates people. These were true performance coaching sessions, as the learner set the agenda and identified and explored their own options.

During the same period, I had meetings with a cross-section of staff and worked extensively with the vice-president and HR representative to look at the bank's performance management processes, asking how these could be adapted and implemented to suit the particular culture of a foreign exchange department. Performance appraisal was compulsory in the bank but there was scope to amend it to suit the style and nature of this specialist department better. I also brought the managers I was coaching into the consultations. I put forward recommendations to adjust the performance appraisal system and completely revised the 360-degree feedback process. These recommendations were accepted, and I was subsequently responsible for their implementation. These tasks comprised pure consultancy, as I first recommended solutions, then had to implement them and, finally, was accountable to the vice-president for the results.

Following this project I switched back to a pure coaching role and carried out one-to-one coaching sessions with the managers and the vice-president on implementing the performance management programme with their staff and their handling of feedback sessions. These sessions were coaching and not training, as they were learner-centred and were about the learner identifying and exploring options – not about me telling them how to do it. Note that, in this assignment, my 'directive', consultant role was complete before I switched to a coaching role. I was therefore able to avoid being too directive in the coaching, since we were not working on *whether* to implement but *how* to implement the scheme, and the skills required that would apply to any scheme.

Following completion of the assignment I evaluated the coaching and the 360-degree feedback, and the results exceeded goals and expectations. We had also, at the outset, established measures of success that were linked to the financial results of the department. These were also exceeded. This was a successful project that produced measurable results. In a dealing environment where people monitor their profit and loss accounts constantly throughout the day, measurable results are important.

However, the example illustrates very well how coaching and consultancy can not only coexist but can support and reinforce each other within a working relationship. In this example, an alternative approach that did not mix consultancy and coaching would have produced an inferior result.

Edgar Schein, an acknowledged expert on leadership and corporate culture, writing about the relationship between coaching and consultancy, sees 'coaching as one kind of intervention (during a consultancy assignment) that may be helpful to clients under certain circumstances. In this context, I think of coaching as establishing a set of behaviours that helps the client to develop a new way of seeing, feeling about and behaving in problematic situations.'[1] This is very much what happened in the assignment described above.

By contrast, to illustrate the consequences of separating coaching from consultancy, it happens frequently in consultancy assignments that clients decide, for example, to engage a consultant to design a new performance appraisal programme and maybe train staff. However, once they see the task as having been finished, they then sever the relationship with the consultant. 'After all,' they argue, 'the job has been completed.' What follows is that the new behaviours have often not been fully assimilated and the whole process flounders, or else people manage the new behaviours to the extent of carrying out the performance appraisal meeting but are not able to convert this into permanent behaviour.

Appraisal then becomes a one-off event, and most of what has been learnt is forgotten until the whole process needs to be repeated some time in the future. Not only does this incur unnecessary expense but it wastes many of the benefits of, in this instance, the appraisal process. Having the opportunity to coach as well as consult means there is a greater likelihood of new behaviours being assimilated and of managers adopting a range of management behaviours that can turn performance appraisal into a range of continuing behaviours that lead to more motivated staff.

Schein also argues that: 'In consultancy, the consultant can never understand the culture of the client system well enough to make accurate diagnoses or provide workable prescriptions. The client owns the problem and is responsible for the solution.'[2] This is yet another reason why the consultant who is also a coach and who uses coaching interventions is likely to be more effective. In the example given above, the coaching ensured that the managers saw the processes through and adapted them, as well as identifying solutions that were workable and that suited them and their environments.

USING COACHING IN CONSULTANCY

Being able to coach is an important but often overlooked skill of the consultant. An example of its importance is provided by a common situation that arises in consultancy when a client actively seeks and expects specific expert advice, only to reject it when it is given. The consultant, in giving this specific advice, may find that the proposed solution does not fit the client's personality, company politics or other situation, and it will be ignored. The client may not be willing to say that they do not understand or agree with the advice offered or that they have already tried it and it doesn't work. This is especially likely to arise if the client feels at all subordinate to the consultant who has, perhaps, greater professional status and expertise.

In these cases, consultants who can use coaching skills will be more effective and will use their coaching skills to establish a helping relationship of equals before they determine what help is needed. In Western cultures that focus on individualism it is often felt to be unacceptable to need help. It implies some inadequacy, or inability to solve a problem. Doing some 'spontaneous coaching', or even setting up a formal coaching relationship within the consultancy assignment may therefore be the most successful way of achieving organisational goals.

If this is the case, it will take particular skills on the part of the consultant to be able to use a range of consultancy and coaching skills. In many ways, it is not unlike the range of skills required for today's HR managers, who need to be both internal consultants and internal coaches.

The overarching goal is to be helpful to the immediate client while being mindful of the impact of interventions on the wider organisation.

Schein emphasises how important it is for both the consultant and the coach to first establish a helping relationship with the client in which the client can safely reveal real, underlying problems. To build this helping relationship, the consultant-coach will need to be in 'process mode'. This involves the consultant-coach surfacing any underlying problems and building a partnership in which the consultant-coach and client take joint responsibility for the outcomes. This helping relationship needs to be built before any guidance, advice or prescriptions are offered.

Schein regards coaching as a subset of consultation and believes the consultant needs to establish this helping relationship to be able to determine the nature of the consultancy that will be offered.

He sees the following three modes of consultancy and the need to choose between them in any given situation. When should the consultant:

- be in 'expert mode', advising a client how to feel, interpret or act in a particular situation?

- act as a 'diagnostician and prescriber', analysing the cause of a problem and proposing a solution?

- be a 'process-oriented' coach who supports and enables the client to gain insight into their situation and the issues they face and to work out for themselves what actions to take or behaviour to modify?

The first two choices demand behaviour that is mostly directive, but the third is quite clearly not.

How the relationship progresses depends on many factors, such as who initiated the process, the status differential between the consultant-coach and the client, whether the client is working on individual or organisational issues and whether the content of the coaching concerns the organisation's goals or organisational processes. In each of these situations, the consultant-coach must be able to move easily between the roles of process consultant, content expert and diagnostician. The ultimate skill of the consultant-coach is to assess the moment-to-moment dynamics of the task and the relationship that will enable them to adopt the appropriate role.

To illustrate these points further, it is helpful to look at some more examples of coaching combined with consultancy.

Dealing with the media is a skill that many senior executives need. It is also a learnable skill. Alex Wise helps businesses communicate with their various audiences so as to enhance and protect their reputation.

According to Wise, companies focus on what they do best: their core business. Too few companies have thought through their potential public relations issues and dealing with the media. From a PR viewpoint, Wise helps businesses focus on the issues that are coming up and the risks they face. He uses coaching to help senior management understand how to deal with the media in difficult circumstances, and how to anticipate what journalists may ask for. He gives one-on-one coaching on dealing with journalists and getting probed and grilled by them.

Many company executives think PR is about writing a press release. In fact, it is more about building and maintaining relationships. Many company executives will at some time find themselves faced with a PR crisis, such as a faulty product or some kind of disaster. A common scenario is when a journalist calls a company for a comment and no one knows who should deal with it or how to handle it properly. Everyone panics. This creates a poor impression with the journalist, who becomes suspicious and may jump to the wrong conclusion.

It is advisable for companies that are likely to be at risk to develop a programme of getting to know journalists to improve chances of getting appropriate and positive media coverage that can build and protect their company's reputation. These things are difficult to deal with and are much easier to handle if the organisation takes a strategic, proactive approach to PR and media.

Wise works on a consultancy basis with organisations, getting them to identify the potential risks to their business and develop PR and media strategies to meet these objectives. In his consultancy work, he finds it is important to understand the client's business objectives and strategies and who the customers are. Sometimes people have such plans prepared and committed to paper, but often they don't, and coaching skills are required to address the issue. Wise does not claim to be a strategy consultant but a consultant who needs to understand the business strategies. He therefore needs to help clients to enunciate their objectives and strategies, which can only be done by applying coaching skills.

Wise also finds that consultancy in his specific area of expertise will be significantly more effective and the PR strategies implemented better if he coaches the people who need to handle these matters to develop skills for dealing with the media. Such skills include being able to get across their story to journalists while avoiding responses that may be taken out of context, misconstrued or misrepresented. These skills require changes in behaviour that can deal with different situations rather than just learned knowledge; each situation will be different and so there is no set of perfect answers that can be memorised.

In coaching, Wise uses case-study examples so that the learner can learn how other people handle particular situations. He uses real-life examples of things that have happened in other companies. Often he calls in journalists to talk about what they do, the problems they encounter and the pressures they are under. Some executives see journalists as uncontrollable tornados who just write what they want. Wise coaches people to develop a mutual understanding with journalists and to appreciate that they need to fill a page with something of interest. When he brings a journalist into a coaching session, they may talk about stories and deadlines to obtain a practical view of the journalist's objectives.

However, practice and role-playing are also important. Wise may set up a scenario where there is a business problem and then someone announces that, say, a reporter from BBC Radio is on the telephone. The client must then deal with this. Afterwards they deconstruct how the learner handled the situation into its various elements and discuss them. The client takes control and leads the discussion. It is important to involve people, getting them to critique themselves, identifying solutions and choosing those they prefer.

He avoids going into expert mode and telling the client how they should have handled matters, for two reasons. First, if Wise tells them what to do they are less likely to assimilate the behaviour than if they realise for themselves what is appropriate. Secondly, there may be different possible ways to handle the issue, and if he gets the client to adopt an approach that the client is not comfortable with, it will be less successful than if the client finds the optimum behaviour for each case.

Wise also coaches people to understand their limitations. Again, a coaching style is far more effective than simply telling someone what they are bad at. Some people become flustered and angry in a media interview. He coaches on how to keep cool, give yourself time, focus on your subject, be clear about the messages and what can you say, and get the facts and figures.

Sometimes Wise may be called in to coach on some specific issues. For example, he has recently coached a chief executive officer to handle rumours of a merger of his business, and a finance director on reporting a problematic financial performance. He often prefers to coach the team, as in this way he helps the management team develop a shared view.

KEY LEARNING POINTS

There are distinct differences between consulting and coaching but, sometimes, it is beneficial to combine the two. This is especially so if the client requires someone to design a process, or give advice and then coach people in how to get the best from it.

In the examples we have seen, the consultant needed to switch between the two roles. Consultancy was needed to give advice and design processes. Coaching was needed to deliver the consultancy message and to help the clients adapt, assimilate the behaviours and deal independently with situations.

The coach does not need to be a consultant, but the consultant who can coach the client when this is appropriate will provide a far better service.

NOTES AND REFERENCES

1   SCHEIN E. (2000) 'Coaching and consultation: Are they the same?' in Goldsmith M., Lyons L. *and* Freas A. (eds) *Coaching for Leadership*. San Francisco, Jossey–Bass.

2   Ibid.

3   Ibid.

7

Using a blend of training and coaching

So far in this book, we have identified some powerful reasons that coaching is a successful learning solution. Training, by contrast, has many shortcomings. Why not give up training courses and set up coaching instead? What can be achieved by using a blend of training and coaching? How are such programmes designed?

WHY NOT GIVE UP TRAINING COURSES AND SET UP COACHING INSTEAD?

Academics and practitioners alike have long been pointing out the limitations of traditional training methodologies, especially classroom training. Research by the German psychologist H. Ebbinghaus[1] produced results that showed that 60 per cent of what is learned in a class is forgotten within one hour and 90 per cent is forgotten within 30 days. In 1998, Roy Harrison of the CIPD reported research from the US, which showed that on average only 10 to 20 per cent of learning through training transfers into people's work.[2] Additionally, the CIPD survey *Workplace Learning in Europe*[3] found that only 16 per cent of respondents rated classroom training as their best way of learning, despite the fact that it was the second most frequently used method after on-the-job training. In their book, *Coaching and Mentoring*, Parsloe and Wray[4] refer to the deficiencies of training to strengthen their advocacy of how coaching and mentoring is a preferable learning method, especially for such topics as personal skills.

In spite of the rather gloomy statistics mentioned above, training continues to be extensively used. Perhaps this bears witness to the advantages a well-constructed and appropriately delivered training course can bring, such as:

- receiving input and advice from an expert
- being able to discuss matters with an expert
- exchanging and developing ideas with colleagues
- having time and space to focus on a particular topic or issue
- practising skills in a 'safe' environment
- creating networks
- learning what goes on in other organisations.

Participating with colleagues on the same in-company training programme also shapes attitudes, creates a company way of doing things, binds people into a team and gives them a shared language. It also enables delegates to get to know others in the organisation and gain insights into their roles.

Nonetheless, deficiencies arise for a multitude of reasons. People work on generic examples and problems in the classroom, and it can be difficult to pick up what is learned and transfer it to their own circumstances. Quite often, people leave training courses with good intentions but then get pulled away from these by the work that has accumulated in their absence. Everyone learns in a different way and at a different pace; some participants may be slower to assimilate new ideas, some may understand the ideas conceptually but find it more difficult to put them into effect. Moreover, it is not possible to change your leadership style in a week. How do you get people to recognise that the best way yesterday is not the best way today? How can you relinquish a controlling style when that has been with you for years?

Often training is run to give people new ways of doing things and new ideas. If there is a lack of integration between the new way and the culture and practices of the organisation, this makes it difficult, if not impossible, to effect change.

BLENDING COACHING WITH TRAINING

The enabling or catalysing effect of coaching can be, as Parsloe and Wray say in *Coaching and Mentoring*, 'the glue that makes the training stick'.[5]

Perhaps the most common way of blending these two learning solutions is for one-to-one coaching to support the transfer of learning from the training room to the workplace, enabling lasting change to be effected. The coach keeps the training alive by helping the learner see through the action plans from the training and practise new behaviours until they become habitual. The coach can also support the learner on an individual basis, by going deeper into the impact the learner has on people around him or her

Mike Travis, a US-based executive coach, provides an example. He works with a large corporate client in the US and provides coaching to delegates as a follow-on from a two- or three-day leadership programme. Travis joins the programme towards the end to introduce himself to the delegates. He briefly meets each person and discusses with them their feedback from the 360-degree and psychometric instruments used on the training. He summarises this feedback with them and identifies the learner's strengths and the areas to cover in the coaching. Sometimes the issues they identify in this first, face-to-face session are not the most crucial to the individual. These often surface later in the coaching, which Travis conducts, mostly, by telephone.

Travis finds that the leadership programme usually takes delegates most of the way to where they want to be. In such cases, Travis sees his role as helping them mull over the learning and relate it to their work situation. Sometimes they need considerably more support, and the coaching surfaces different and deeper issues.

Dave is a senior manager with a multinational, fast-moving consumer goods company. He recently attended an in-house senior leadership development programme and was given coaching as part of the follow-up to this. The overall aim was to establish a coaching style of management as the prevalent style in the organisation. The training enabled Dave to gain insights into the impact of his leadership style and also his style as a colleague and teamplayer. Of great value were the networking opportunities. Dave believes that whereas the training raised his awareness of the issues, it was the coaching that actually enabled him to adopt the new behaviours and become more 'flexible in his approach and get more engagement from people'. Dave received one-and-a-half days and three telephone calls of coaching over a six-month period.

An international telecommunications company has combined coaching with training in a rather different format. At the turn of the millennium, this company was undergoing a major transformation. Its business strategy focused on the organisation transforming from a traditional telecommunications company into a communications company operating in the new advanced markets of multimedia and the Internet. As part of the drive to achieve this strategy, a leadership programme was developed. The purpose of the programme was to promote and cultivate a healthy, high-performing organisational culture. The content focused on the 'how' rather than the 'what' of leadership.

The organisation was particularly keen to do something to look after executive talent. The aim was to achieve a balance between delivering commercial imperatives and maximising the sustainable potential of the people. It was ethical and forward-thinking. It was a high-quality initiative aimed at the top.

The programme was run for functional teams so that they had the shared experience to encourage the translation of the learning back into the workplace. It incorporated a balance of assessment, coaching and shared team events. Coaching and training were interwoven throughout.

In the first part of the programme, the coaches spent significant time with the team leader understanding their needs, personally and for the team, and customising the programme to meet their specific aims. The coaches also worked on a one-to-one basis with the team leader and each team member, building rapport, identifying the issues to be worked on and gaining an understanding of the environment. From the delegates' point of view, this gave them the opportunity to reflect on the challenges they were facing, how they worked together with others, their strengths, and what they wanted to get out of the team training event. The leader and coach also clarified the roles they would each take during the team events. These were that the leader remained the leader and the coach focused on helping delegates explore new thinking.

The whole team then came together for an event, which would have been at least a 'long' day but sometimes extended over two-and-a-half days. The team included the entire group; everyone part of the decision-making process for that board or team would be there. Usually this included the HR and financial representatives.

A characteristic of the programme was that people worked through real issues, blurring the distinction between the event and their normal operating environment. In addition, there were a number of models and philosophies that underpinned the training and that encouraged a common culture throughout the organisation. These were primarily around personal effectiveness and leadership, and reflected the style of leadership to which the company aspired.

During the event, the coaches aimed to cultivate an environment that encouraged people to step back from their usual day-to-day activities and concerns. The coaches acted as guides, sharing models and experiences that enabled the team to consider and reflect on their own performance, beliefs and assumptions.

After the event, the team members were encouraged to start applying the learning. If they wished, one of the programme's coaches would support them on a one-to-one basis. Sometimes, individuals or indeed the whole team requested support with a key issue.

The coach who carried out the pre-event work also facilitated the event and worked with the team or with individuals afterwards to ensure consistency.

The first phase of implementation of this programme, spanning the board and each of their leadership teams, was designed and delivered by organisational change consultants. However, it was considered critical to bring the learning within the organisation and to develop an in-house coaching capability to share the programme beyond the very top. Ten senior operational managers who had a predisposition to coaching were identified. These managers were trained to become coaches and it was intended that coaching activities would take up 20 per cent of their time. It took four weeks of intensive training over a period of five to six months. The time in between the training was intended to enable the trainees to consolidate what they had learned and start putting it into practice.

The people selected and trained to be coaches on this programme had a genuine desire to want to help everyone make a difference and strongly believed in the emphasis on personal development.

The value of the programme was assessed in terms of the perception of how the teams were working together, back in their functional roles and as a leadership team after the programme. In addition, a number of the teams chose to repeat the use of a Leadership Behaviours Inventory, which was one of the key models used in the training, in order to understand how the way they were perceived had shifted.

For customers of the programme, referral and further requests for support also provided feedback on the value placed on the investment by the participants.

Evaluation of the initiative showed that customising the content and style to focus on the specific needs of the team was critical to the success of the programme. It also increased the value of the event for delegates and lay the foundations of rapport and mutual understanding.

The feedback from the internal coaches indicates that they valued the opportunity their role gave them to meet people across the organisation and to contribute to helping both individuals and the business succeed.

CASE STUDY

The Public Service Leaders Scheme

The Public Service Leaders Scheme (PSLS) demonstrates blended learning in a different context. The programme combines coaching, mentoring, e-learning and classroom training, as well as other learning solutions.

The programme aims to develop leaders across the public sector and the civil service. It is targeted at those who expect to move to senior leadership positions within the next three to five years. The PSLS is part of the Public Service Reform Agenda and is run by the Cabinet Office. The programme is a collaborative venture between the civil service, local authorities, the NHS and the police. It is the only scheme that embraces the whole of the public service and seeks to develop individuals and organisations.

The scheme draws people together from across all parts of the public sector to network and learn about the different working cultures and share good practice and the challenges of leadership. This is given further impetus through a part of the programme (known as interchange) that requires delegates to work in a different part of the public sector.

The PSLS is a development programme that aims to provide participants with:

- better understanding of connections, cultures and practices across the public sector

- the skills and experience needed for senior leadership positions, including new strategies for tackling complex issues in their employing organisation, allowing them to provide better services to the public

- increased confidence and knowledge when working with colleagues and service users from other public-service organisations.

The scheme is based on action learning, underpinned with theoretical study that can be accredited by Birmingham University at postgraduate certificate level. Each participant draws up their own individual learning contract for the programme with the support of their sponsor, a mentor and a personal organisation and development manager (POD), who also helps participants make the best of all of the resources at their disposal through the scheme.

The programme itself is flexible and delegates may follow it for between one and three years.

What does the programme look like?

Each of the six elements works in different ways:

Foundation event

A two-day residential event to identify learning goals providing tools and strategies to develop self-awareness.

Figure 7 | *Crystal diagram showing components of Public Service Leaders Scheme*

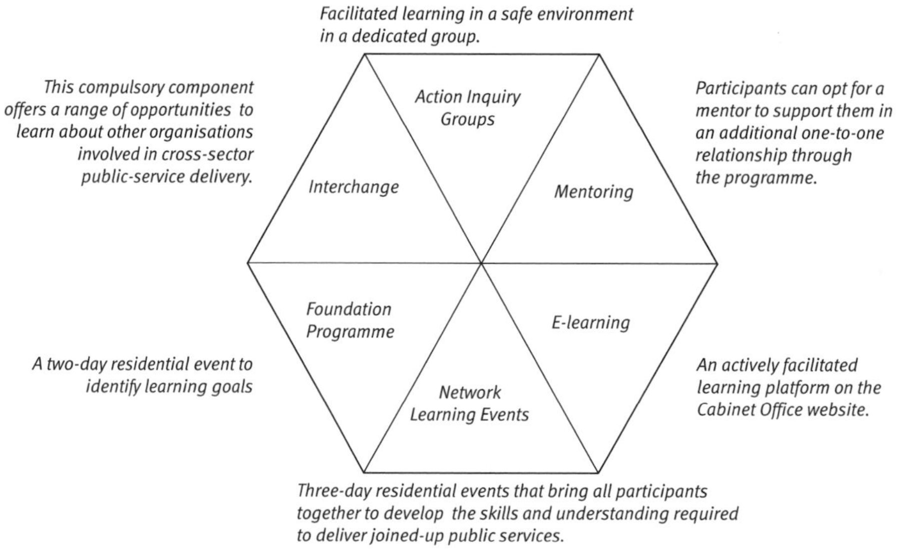

Facilitated learning in a safe environment in a dedicated group.

This compulsory component offers a range of opportunities to learn about other organisations involved in cross-sector public-service delivery.

Participants can opt for a mentor to support them in an additional one-to-one relationship through the programme.

Action Inquiry Groups

Interchange

Mentoring

Foundation Programme

E-learning

Network Learning Events

A two-day residential event to identify learning goals

An actively facilitated learning platform on the Cabinet Office website.

Three-day residential events that bring all participants together to develop the skills and understanding required to deliver joined-up public services.

Network learning event

Three-day events that bring all participants together to develop the skills and understanding required to deliver joined-up public services, including partnership and collaborative working, community leadership and political sensitivity.

E-learning

An actively facilitated learning platform provided for participants to continuously share experiences, key learning points and current challenges.

Mentoring

Participants can choose to have a mentor to support them through the scheme and beyond.

Action inquiry groups

Facilitated learning in a safe environment in a dedicated group to develop leadership skills aided by peers.

Interchange

This compulsory component offers a range of opportunities to learn about other organisations involved in cross-sector public-service delivery and to gain new skills and experiences identified in their individual learning contracts.

Benefits of the programme

The thrust of the programme is to develop deep personal learning about how to shift style from management to leadership. It also puts across the scope of public services, widening participants' views of the complexity of issues in the public sector. The final desired outcome is to develop a group of leaders who will ensure improved public-service delivery by developing partnership projects across the public sector.

Foundation programme and learning contract

The Foundation programme is the first part of the scheme, when participants start drawing up their learning contracts. In these contracts, delegates identify short-terms goals (1 – 3 years) and then later, as they progress through the programme, they identify mid- and long-terms goals. It generally takes delegates six months to finalise their goals, and they receive one-to-one coaching support from the PODs to help them. In this way, delegates gain exposure to different areas and disciplines, broaden their outlook and get to know about opportunities they previously had not considered, or even known about. They are then able to set goals based on this different perspective and understanding. The coaching support is regarded as vital to encouraging people to develop their ideas and to make sure the goals they set are sufficiently challenging and stretching to get them to where they want to go.

The PODs also work with each participant on their feedback from the Team Leadership Questionnaire, a 360-degree feedback tool focused on public-service leadership and specifically designed for British public servants.

As participants move across the 'crystal', their learning takes place in different kinds of relationship.

Mentoring

Participants are matched with a mentor, with whom they have a one-to-one relationship. As well as acting as a critical friend and sounding board throughout the programme, the mentor will also help the learner make the transition to and from the sector to which they will be assigned while undertaking the interchange part of the programme. Mentors help learners come to grips with the new culture.

The scheme is proposing to provide increased support to the mentors, possibly in the form of a 'meta' mentor to whom mentors can turn for confidential support and mentoring. Training is provided for the mentors.

Action inquiry group

For this part of the programme, participants work in small groups on issues that they often have in common – for example, how to manage asylum seekers across the system. They look at a range of issues and problems that arise in different parts of the public sector and learn about cultural differences.

These action inquiry groups comprise people with diverse backgrounds and from different levels in their respective organisations. This helps participants develop insights into the benefits of diversity and the advantages of partnership projects.

Network learning event

This event is run along the lines of a traditional classroom event. It covers leadership theory and the current theory of partnership working. Participants work on case studies, discuss hot topics and coach one another.

How they know if the scheme is successful

It is too early to measure the impact of the scheme. There is, however, some anecdotal evidence coming through. For example, one participant has set up a partnership in his area between the local authority, the NHS and the police force on how to handle asylum seekers. This participant has found that through just one year on the scheme he has learned to appreciate the benefits of partnering and understand how to influence and share information and knowledge.

The scheme also regards the very low drop-out rate experienced to date as an early measure of success.

KEY LEARNING POINTS

Blending training and coaching can be immensely powerful, especially at times of organisational transformation where people need to change their behaviours and leadership styles. It enables learners to achieve the benefits of working together and also to have help and support with their own personal issues. Such one-to-one support also helps them transfer the learning to the workplace until it becomes habitual.

A mix of training and coaching is also beneficial for programmes aimed at team development. It enables team members to gain the advantages of working together, and at the same time ensures their individual needs are supported. Customising each training event through coaching support at the outset gives each individual the opportunity to identify the aims, values and behaviours they want for their team.

One-to-one coaching, especially when it is added to the costs of training, is an expensive option. It is, therefore, imperative to ensure that the benefits will outweigh the costs.

A valuable learning point from all the above examples is that coaching needs to be provided at the point where it is the most beneficial. In developing the programme, identify the aims, the skills and the knowledge areas that are critical to success, but that people might have the most difficulty adopting, and aim the coaching at these. In some cases, this might be the transfer of learning after the training.

In the PSLS, coaching support at an early stage helped delegates develop the broader perspectives required for setting learning goals that would challenge, stimulate and extend the individual's horizons.

NOTES AND REFERENCES

1   HOHN R. (1995) *Classroom learning and teaching.* New York, Longman Publishing.

2   www.oscm.co.uk/resources/articles/oscm_res_istraining.htm

3   Chartered Institute of Personnel and Development (2001) *Workplace learning in Europe.* London, CIPD.

4   PASCOE E. *and* WRAY M. (2000) *Coaching and Mentoring.* London, Kogan Page.

5   Ibid.

8

Online coaching

In this chapter, the exciting opportunities for online coaching are explored. These opportunities are inextricably linked to successful online learning, so this broader context is also considered.

What impact has e-learning had so far? What advantages does it offer? What considerations need to be incorporated into an e-learning strategy? What roles can e-coaching take? What are the skills required of the coach in this context? What of executive coaching? Can that be carried out online? In answer to this last question, I report on an online coaching initiative that has been developed by Sfera Gruppo Enel for the Enel Group of Companies in Italy.

Before going any further, it may be helpful to clarify that throughout this chapter the term online and the prefix 'e-' are used interchangeably. Strictly speaking, they are different insofar as the first is commonly understood to utilise the power of the Internet while the second only requires a computer on which to run software. For our purposes, however, the difference between the two does not affect our two central themes: how to create successful online learning and the role of the online coach.

WHAT IMPACT HAS E-LEARNING HAD SO FAR?

Studies conducted on both sides of the Atlantic indicate that progress to date on implementing e-learning has been patchy. It certainly has not yet made the impact many expected. There are several possible reasons but they seem, mostly, to arise from a widespread fear – or, at least, apprehension – of technology, together with inadequate computer skills among much of the workforce and slow Internet download speeds. The notion of taking time during the working day to 'learn' in this manner requires many people to adopt a different mindset. This is especially true for managers who need to trust their staff to take time out to learn and still get the day-to-day job done. The high cost of implementing e-learning is another major consideration that has held back development.

These factors are likely to matter less as organisations upgrade their technology, as more workers gain access to workstations and broadband, and as familiarity, training and practice lead people to develop their computer skills. The uncertain economic climate of the early twenty-first century has caused many delays in new technology investment, but opinion among forecasters in the IT industry is that organisations cannot delay for much longer – if only because of the natural economic life of computers and networks: within five or six years of purchase, computers become less reliable and their specifications rapidly fall behind the demands of more modern applications. We seem likely, therefore, to see significant upgrading activity within the next few years. As the obstacles to e-learning disappear, so the break-even point at which e-learning begins to cost less than alternative solutions, such as classroom training, will come down. In turn, this will make e-learning a more viable option in many more circumstances.

There are already indications that online learning is increasing. The latest American Society for Training and Development (ASTD) *State of the Industry Report* predicts that by 2004 its benchmark organisations will be delivering 25 per cent of their training through new technology.[1] Companies such as Dow Chemical and Ford Motor have recently announced major cost savings achieved through e-learning programmes. In the UK, the CIPD[2] has worked with 11 organisations on the practical issues they are facing in implementing e-learning and how they can overcome them. There is considerable optimism that these programmes will be successful. The report resulting from this work offers some valuable learning, and a summary of the conclusions is set out in Appendix 1 at the end of this book. Moreover, a recent survey (commissioned by ICUS, an international e-learning consultancy, in partnership with HR Gateway)[3] found that, of 625 respondents, the majority had conducted e-learning trials, and 55 per cent of the respondents viewed it as a success.

WHAT ADVANTAGES DOES ONLINE LEARNING OFFER?

E-learning as a medium offers many advantages to learners and organisations alike. Key ones are:

Cost and time savings

The learner does not need to give up a job or travel to a remote location in order to study. The tutors also can work from any convenient location, and their work can be stored and recycled many times.

Choosing your time for learning

The learner and tutors can choose their times for learning and teaching, fitting them around other commitments. This is made possible by activities such as discussion groups, notice boards, e-mail and self-paced interactive programs.

Sharing and questioning

Interaction and debate can be added via e-mail, discussion groups, chat rooms, virtual tutorials and phone lines to experts. This introduces a social element to the learning; it can also help the learner put the learning into their organisational context.

Real time/Space-shifting

The technology allows the opportunity to meet in live online tutorials with experts. This allows many learners to participate in practical exercises. It also enables many people to benefit from the knowledge and experience of others.

Collaboration

Possibly one of the most exciting potential uses of the Internet is the ability for professionals to work together and pool expertise from all corners of the world, or indeed from all corners of the same organisation. One high-tech company that develops software for personal organisers and handheld devices has found that its internal discussion group enables any employee to put forward ideas or help solve problems in connection with the development of its products. This enables the company to develop better products, and faster than before. The discussion thread also serves as a learning tool for those working on different products or from different disciplines, broadening their knowledge and understanding.

Social interaction

Many people believe that the Internet is impersonal. There is a notion of the e-learner or the Internet user being a nerdy individual who shuns personal contact. This is far from the truth. There are many social aspects to being online. Louis Searchwell and Doug King, both of whom are e-learning specialists, find that people migrate towards one another online. People find common interests, make friends and support each other by sharing ideas and information and jointly solving problems. E-mail, of course, enables many people to stay in touch and draw on one another's business experiences. All of these options can be valuable learning opportunities.

WHAT NEEDS TO BE INCORPORATED INTO AN E-LEARNING STRATEGY, AND WHAT IS THE ROLE OF THE COACH?

E-learning can, of course, take many different forms. It can be developed in-house or be externally supplied. It may be a structured, interactive program that someone will work through on an individual basis or it may involve bringing together, online, a community of learners with shared interests and a common purpose.

Deciding which e-learning programs to invest in requires a strategy in itself. However, this is outside our remit here, where I am concerned with how to ensure that the e-learning the organisation has invested in is successful.

An e-learning strategy should identify such issues as: what business needs the e-learning program is to satisfy, who it is for, what will motivate them to complete it, how it is to be organised and promoted and how it might blend in with other learning solutions. The use of a coach and coaching techniques can be enormously effective in assisting an organisation to formulate such an e-learning strategy and in supporting its implementation. This is because the answers to the sort of 'soft', judgemental issues involved in such questions are almost certainly latent within an executive team. This executive team are already familiar with the business issues, culture and individuals, but may need help in vocalising and analysing the solutions.

Identifying the business issues and keeping the learner motivated

The success of any e-learning initiative depends upon learner motivation, which is at its highest on activities that people feel will help them do their jobs better, assist their promotion aspirations and which they can readily link to business goals. A coach can play an important role in enthusing a learner, assisting them to identify personal and organisational needs and supporting them through difficult periods in their learning.

A coach can help learners determine their learning needs and identify their learning styles and preferences. A coach can then source suitable online materials and programs. When there is a specific program in mind, a few penetrating questions can uncover whether the program suits the learner and what will motivate them to see it through:

- What do you hope to get out of the program?
- What are your interests in the topic?
- What problems have you encountered with this topic?

Answers to these questions will also enable the coach to support the learner throughout the program, by keeping them focused on their objectives.

(Note: These questions are similarly valuable at the design stage, to ensure that the program will meet learner needs. The ARCS model of motivation is also appropriate to the development of e-learning programs. This model is explained in Chapter 10 in the section on motivation.)

The coach can also draw to the learner's attention how the program links to business needs, thus clarifying for the learner how their efforts will be rewarded.

The coach will be helped in this endeavour if e-learning is supported by the top people in the organisation. Many online learning programs have flopped because people had no compelling reason to use it and there was no appetite from the top to sell the concept as an important one. Conversely, the CEO at the Prudential has been a huge advocate of a system they set up a couple of years ago, and it has been very successful there.

Working through the program

Learners benefit from having someone to support them as they work through a program, and here again a coach has a crucial role. A coach can provide support on three levels: technology, motivation and content.

Technology

Here the coach helps the new user of online learning to use the system and overcome any technical obstacles that arise. This can be provided through an IT help-desk, although the help-desk will need to understand the system in its broader aspects, such as navigation, testing and interactivity rather than just the technology. A well-designed program will provide some on-screen support but this has its limitations, and many learners prefer to talk to someone about their problems.

Motivation

A good coach will be readily available to help people along and, through a positive approach, will enable them to use the program to best advantage.

Content

Depending on the type and nature of the learning, it may be appropriate for a program to have subject coaches, as well as a co-ordinator-coach who can answer people's queries and identify further materials or information sources.

The learner may need to carry out some preparation before undertaking the online learning program. As they progress through the e-learning, they may also make action plans that need to be followed through afterwards. The coach can play a valuable role in supporting the learner in these instances too.

For all these roles, the coach is preferably an offline coach who is a member of the organisation. The roles could, however, be performed by an online coach who works with learners individually on a specific program, or who works with an online community of learners who are all undergoing the same program.

Identifying a learning community and determining their needs

As we discussed earlier, online learning can take many forms. It can be an interactive, structured program that someone works through individually, or it can involve bringing together a community of learners with shared interests and a common purpose. This community may be from the same organisation, or several.

Searchwell and King, who develop and advise on online learning, believe that a coach can have a major role in identifying the online community and keeping them together. In one practical example from their experience, they sent out two e-mails to set up an online learning community for a specific academic topic, which brought in a surprising 60 responses. They then worked with these people to identify their needs as well as what would keep them interested. The program was developed around these expressed needs and ran successfully for some time. People were motivated because they had a reason to be there, and they all saw they stood to gain significantly from sharing information and ideas and from brainstorming.

Jo Ayoubi, who also develops and advises on online learning, believes the role of the coach is to bring people together, to moderate discussions and facilitate live debates or live learning sessions. If someone cannot participate in the live discussion, you can record it and send it to them, or rerun it. You can also save it for yourself to refer back to at a later date. Ayoubi reports that:

> *The best example of having a coach for online learning was when I was studying for my own e-learning qualification. The coach, who was also the tutor, was available to answer phone calls at particular times and days of the week, and I used this facility a number of times. We also had a bulletin board where people could post questions to the group, which led to peer-to-peer coaching. The coach was also available to answer e-mail queries from students. A number of live online sessions were run using a 'chat room' facility, though these were a little limited, as people needed to be online at the same time, and some people experienced technical problems when they first started to use the service.*

Online relationships can bring people together from within the same company or they can bring people together from other organisations. There are advantages to be had from both, in much the same way as from attending an in-house or an open training course.

Organising online learning

How e-learning is organised and introduced into the organisation is also crucial to ensuring its success. A coach may include these responsibilities within his or her overall remit, or they may be performed by someone else.

The learning environment

Many organisations have found that best results are achieved when learners are able to choose where to learn. This may be at their desk, in a learning centre, at home, or indeed in an in-company refreshment area, albeit that this last location will need to be a quiet area to minimise distractions.

Time to learn is also important. Surrey County Council, one of the organisations featured in the CIPD study,[4] asked every learner and their manager to complete a learning contract that commits the learners to two hours a week of work time to undertake a particular e-learning program. Other organisations prefer a more fluid arrangement based on trust. What is important is that learners are free to choose when and where to learn and for how long. Everyone has their own preferences. For example, some people may like to work in a concentrated manner and complete a whole program at one sitting, while others may wish to complete the program over several sessions.

Online learning is particularly effective when people can integrate it into their daily work. For example, people may use e-learning at the time they are carrying out performance appraisals. The system needs to be designed so that it will help them prepare for and carry out performance appraisal meetings with their staff but, if the learner is interested, it will also help them dig deeper into issues such as motivation.

Learners need support. We have already identified the importance of a coach in supporting learners with issues concerning technology, content and motivation. The line manager also has an important role in supporting the learner by discussing and encouraging, giving recognition to the learner for having completed the program and incorporating it into performance review and other processes.

Online learning is more easily accepted in a 'collaborative' culture of trust and empowerment than in a command-and-control culture where managers react against the idea of people being allowed to use the Internet freely and organise their own time and work schedules. HR managers and coaches will need to keep this in mind when they are launching e-learning. In command-and-control environments it is likely to be more successful, at least initially, to introduce compulsory e-learning. This might be a program that the learner must undertake to fulfil the demands of the job, such as to meet regulatory requirements. Learners should also be given 'official' or contractual time for this learning.

Introducing the system

Simply building e-learning is no guarantee that learners will come; time and effort also need to be invested in marketing the initiative. The following guidelines are based on those contained in a report by Brandon-Hall.com,[5] a research firm in Sunnyvale, California:

- Research audience needs, and design and present e-learning to show how it meets these needs.

- Pay attention to culture in the way you package and present e-learning. For instance, don't offer prizes for completing a program unless this fits with your way of doing things.

- Be specific about what the e-learning is designed to achieve. Explain the specific training opportunities and advantages it offers to particular groups of staff, rather than presenting it as a boon to the company in general.

- Obtain management support and find internal e-learning champions who can spread the word. Support at the highest level is crucial.

- Brand your program so that it has the look and feel of your company. Avoid jargon and make sure all case studies and other materials are relevant.

- Keep communicating. Collect hard facts and anecdotal evidence to show how successful the e-learning program is and to show how you are acting on feedback from learners. Publish this widely on noticeboards, in newsletters, at team briefings etc.

- Tie e-learning into other processes. For example, make sure recognition is given to completion of e-learning at performance appraisal, etc.

Program design

A key finding from the ICUS/HR Gateway survey referred to earlier is that 'coaching and content rule the day'. A total of 94 per cent of the respondents singled out 'customised content' as crucial to controlling the success of online learning; and 82 per cent of the respondents felt that an e-coach has a 'critical role' in enabling content to be customised and put in context, as well as increasing the learners' motivation to acquire and share knowledge.

Searchwell and King have found from their research and experiences that people remember things better from online learning and get more out of it. But the learning environment needs to be right for them. It needs to be learner-centred, not technology-led.

Martyn Sloman of the CIPD also believes strongly that in the future programs should be learner-centred. In a joint paper he wrote with Jennifer Taylor, 'Customising the learning experience for Human Resource Decisions International, 2002'[6] he advances the view that a program should be customised to the organisation and personalised to the individual.

Customisation allows for the material to be presented in the company format, with company logos and learners' names inserted at appropriate stages. It also allows for learner tracking. Customisation can ensure that each learner covers the material that they, or the company, need to have covered. Typically a course menu would be presented to indicate the learning appropriate to the individual's level or position or their previous learning experiences. Links to other material will also be suggested. Content will also be customised, and case studies, exercises and other materials will be relevant and based on the activities and culture of the organisation. Attention too will be paid to tone and wording, as people get irritated if these are alien to what they are used to.

Personalising learning is about designing the program so that it suits the individual's learning style and preferences. Through personalisation, programs would allow for the screens to be altered to reflect a learner's preference for different sorts of information or different layouts. It would also offer topics in different formats so that the learner can choose whether to learn by discussing with others, reading, working through exercises, listening, or using a mixture of these.

For example, some people want to retain the option of looking at all the text. Other people, however, prefer social interaction and find it helpful to visit a chat room or discussion group where discussing experiences can reinforce more theoretical lessons learnt elsewhere in the program.

While Sloman and Taylor found a great deal of activity on customisation, they conclude there is little evidence to date of progress on personalisation. This differentiation between customisation and personalisation is immensely useful for the coach to keep in mind when working on the design and development of a program, and when sourcing online programs and materials for learners.

Blended learning

Online learning and coaching are increasing access to learning for everyone by breaking down barriers: cost, time, availability, effort and so on.

These developments present HR and training managers with opportunities to craft creative, cost-effective learning solutions that combine the different uses of new technologies with traditional classroom training and traditional coaching and mentoring. Known increasingly as 'blended learning', this offers an opportunity to provide a mix of learning methods tailored to the individual's learning style and preferences, the needs of the organisation and the circumstances in which the learning is taking place.

In her book, *Web-Based Training*,[7] Dr Margaret Driscoll bases blended learning on four concepts. I have used these to create the following framework, which I hope will help the HR and training professional design a blended learning initiative.

Framework for blended learning

Combine or mix:

1 different modes of web-based technology, such as live virtual classroom, self-paced instruction, collaborative learning, streaming video, audio and text

2 different ways of learning: build into the program options for individuals to tailor the learning method to suit their preferred ways of learning

3 instructional technology (videotape, CD-Rom, web-based training, film) with face-to-face, instructor-led training or one-to-one coaching

4 instructional technology with actual job tasks in order to create a harmonious effect of learning and working.

Some ideas of how blended learning can work can be suggested:

- Deliver assessments and pre-work online. Material can be tailored to the individual by testing knowledge and understanding. Instead of merely offering 'dumb links' from one page of text to another, the software can direct the learner to the page or moving image that is appropriate, based upon their rate of progress, degree of understanding etc. For example, the learner may take an online test to gauge progress, the results of which can switch them to a remedial route or an advanced, more challenging route.

- Make reference materials available. Combine these with practical exercises. At the moment, the Internet provides a wealth of information in the form of pages that are read, as from a book. The technology permits searching through a vast index of material available throughout the world, in many different languages, and also enables printing out at any remote location. As mentioned previously, most e-learning is still based on learning by understanding, or the cognitive theory of learning, putting across content, in much the same way as a book. However, this is no more than the surface of e-learning. The technology provides tremendous scope for adding extra layers of sophistication to learning that is not available from books. An e-learning package can be designed that is interactive; it can also be personalised to suit the individual's learning preferences. I do not mean by this just the 'welcome back, Janice' that flashes up on the screen. Rather, it can deliver material in different formats, using the printed word, diagrams, sound, moving images etc, so that it caters to a mix of all learning styles. At the same time, the choice of style of delivery can be left in the hands of the learner to switch between media.

- Links to higher levels of detail can be offered to more able learners, to stimulate wider thinking and deepen knowledge.

- Provide online support: learners often appreciate help from a real person who can answer questions, help learners devise strategies for learning or provide moral support.

- Deliver classroom training or one-to-one coaching.

- Follow up with online communities of practice: creating a threaded discussion for learners to access, or set up chat rooms or virtual classrooms.

- Use mentoring or coaching as a tool to extend the classroom experience and help with the transfer of learning.

- Access experts: as a follow-up to classroom training or online learning, a live virtual classroom program can be created to provide learners with access to the experts in a remote location, or with an opportunity to get answers quickly from the best sources.

- Maximise e-mail and messaging: this can be used to include new information, pose and answer questions, send reminders and so on.

Monitoring and evaluation

It is important to monitor and evaluate e-learning to ensure it achieves its aims and provides value for money. (For more on evaluation see Chapter 9.) The technology should facilitate evaluation because the learner can be tested, and progress through the material can be tracked online. Tracking should also reveal whether the learner is engaging with the material and learning new skills or assimilating knowledge.

However, the final test cannot be mediated by technology: it is whether the learning has been assimilated and applied. Colleagues, subordinates and line managers may help to evaluate this but a significant element of assessment must come from the learner: is the program value for money? As with offline learning and coaching, someone must make a value judgement: is the individual performing better? Is the organisation performing better? If yes, is it owing to the learning programme?

WHO SHOULD PERFORM THE COACHING ROLE?

Online learning and coaching offer significant opportunities to many people to extend their skills and responsibilities. HR and training professionals are ideally placed to take on some of the coaching roles described above, especially those for identifying and building the community and motivating learners. They may also be subject coaches, where appropriate. IT people can, obviously, take on the role of coach to support learners in their use of the technology, but they too can take on the other roles of building and maintaining the community, motivating learners and acting as subject coach. All these roles can be development opportunities for individuals throughout the organisation. It is recommended that the coach be outside the learning community, so as to be able to maintain an independent viewpoint.

What skills are required of the coach?

The coach needs to understand how people learn and what motivates them.

Good communication skills are also essential. Precision with words and language are exceptionally important in on-screen communication, and the coach needs to be keenly aware of this and be able to advise learners, especially when they are participating in discussion groups or chat rooms.

The coach must have the same interpersonal and relationship-building skills expected of the more traditional coach. Whether online or offline, coaching demands the ability to work with individuals to understand their needs, maintain their motivation and support them through problems.

There are many instances where coaches may work with people in different countries. An understanding of cultural differences and how this affects the way people behave and do business will enhance the coach's ability to build the community, motivate the learner and deal with issues they raise.

The coach must also be patient and permit people to learn at their own pace. Some people will be quicker than others, and the online environment needs to allow for this, as does the coach. The coach needs to watch what is going on and keep learners focused in the right direction while monitoring each learner individually, assessing their progress and intervening to redirect or assist them.

The coach must understand a wide variety of issues. As well as being a content expert, they need to understand how the online course has been designed, what its objectives are, how people are working through the material, what is being tested, and the external factors affecting the learners. The corporate coach also needs to understand the cultural and process issues affecting the learners. Finally, the coach should have some understanding of the technology (unless there is a well-informed help-desk available) to be able to help out the learners when something goes wrong with the program.

The online coach working with a community also needs to have excellent facilitation skills. It requires considerable skill and practice to facilitate a group of people you cannot see and ensure everyone gets a full chance to participate.

Whether the coach is from within the organisation or is an online coach, the program needs to be designed so that, between them, the coach and the software track the learner – for example, by showing when and how often the learner uses the program, how long they connect for and what stage they have reached in their learning. This is valuable information for the coach to identify the level of support the learner requires.

There are some indications that learning systems are being developed to produce 'intelligence' such as different learner preferences. This still seems to be some way off, but when it is available it will enable the coach to work with the learner to identify their learning methods and then adapt the program to suit these.

The academic and medical worlds have, on the whole, been quicker to grasp the benefits of technology than the commercial world. Perhaps this is because many commercial firms tend to be secretive? True e-learning is collaborative.

The International Virtual Medical School (IVIMEDS) is an interesting example of cross-border collaboration. As societies demand ever-improving health care, so time pressures on medical training increase. All medical schools throughout the world face similar problems. Resources are stretched as student numbers expand and the curriculum is extended as medical knowledge increases. The IVIMEDS launch brochure suggests that medical schools are faced with a number of challenges and that collaboration using e-learning must form part of the response.

These challenges are identified as: transforming how students learn; sharing expertise and resources; delivering a high-quality and financially sustainable programme; increasing access to medical education (this challenge has immense implications for the assistance of less developed countries); working in partnership with continuing education; and providing leadership in medical education.

The IVIMEDS project is an example of how people can work together online to develop the learning program and how students can then form learning communities as they work through it. In both cases, it is possible to identify roles for coaches, both online coaches and coaches who work with the student in situ, at their medical school, motivating them to learn, coaching them where necessary in connection with their online work, helping them reflect on their learning, incorporating their online learning into their practical experience, organising any classroom training and setting up learning communities.

EXECUTIVE COACHING

So far I have looked at the different coaching roles that are available through the use of e-learning materials. What of executive coaching? Can that be carried out online?

At first glance, it may seem that online coaching has significantly less to offer than other forms of coaching. Neither video-conferencing nor webcams are appropriate learning environments for conversations that are 'intimate' and that involve strict confidentiality, as is required in executive coaching. I can envisage circumstances, however, where e-coaching may be successfully combined with one-to-one coaching. For instance, during a telephone coaching relationship where coach and learner have a specific need to work through documents together, that part of the coaching could use a webcam and microphone on the computer.

The technology offers two alternative ways of working: synchronous, where people work together at the same time, asynchronous, where people work together but at different times. Most coaches who carry out face-to-face coaching offer telephone helplines and use e-mail for reminders, for exchanging bits of news or information between sessions, or for agreeing the next agenda and discussing progress. This can be extended, and often is, to asynchronous, spontaneous coaching, so that problem and questions and responses and suggestions can be transmitted back and forth without the necessity of the two people being available at exactly the same time.

The case study that follows shows how one organisation is using, very effectively, the online environment for performance coaching.

CASE STUDY

Sfera Gruppo Enel

Action plan showing menu options for setting out learning needs (top box) and how these will be met (lower box)

Figure 8 | *Sfera – screen shot of action plan*

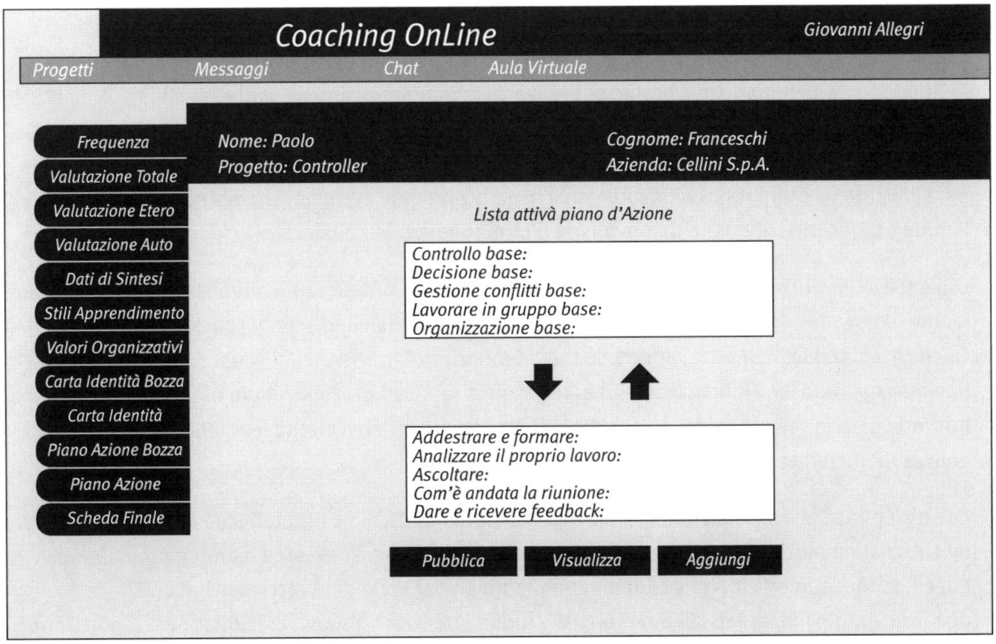

Enel is one of Italy's major industrial conglomerates, employing 75,000 people and comprising five divisions and numerous subsidiary companies. One of these companies is Sfera. Set up in 1999 as Enel's corporate university, Sfera is responsible for training and development for the entire group. It designs and delivers a wide range of learning and development initiatives, including an extensive range of innovative online distance learning programmes which boast some 25,000 registered users. The depth, breadth and variety of these distance learning systems have formed an excellent basis from which Sfera has now developed an online performance coaching programme.

Sfera has been arranging face-to-face coaching for groups of Enel employees for some time. In spite of the success that most individual coaching assignments have achieved, Antonella d'Apruzzo, Sfera's Training and Job Orientation Manager, has found many line and HR managers reluctant to champion coaching as a learning solution for their staff. This reluctance stems mainly from line managers seeing coaching as too costly but also because they are wary about whether the coaching will be geared sufficiently to organisational needs. D'Apruzzo, together with her team and a firm of consultants, Asset Management, has spent 15 months developing an online coaching initiative that will overcome these problems while retaining the advantages of traditional face-to-face performance coaching.

Learners will be sponsored for the coaching programme by their line managers and local head of HR. The reasons they are likely to be put forward might be because they are taking on their first management role, because they are high-potential employees requiring a fast-track development programme or perhaps because of some organisational transformation.

The first stage of the programme is analysis. Learners complete a range of self-analysis instruments which explore their behaviour and impact on others in a range of areas, such as leadership, team-building, problem-solving, etc. Their line managers also input into these instruments, which produce a profile of the learners' strengths and weaknesses. This profile is then matched to an organisational competency framework. The process is automated and is based on tests and questionnaires that have been developed precisely to Enel's own requirements but are similar to or compatible with commonly used proprietary systems. Learners also complete a learning styles questionnaire that is based on the theories of Kolb.

Once these instruments have been completed, the system produces an automated profile of the learner, known as an 'identity card', which the coach analyses and then discusses with the learner. Once coach and learner have agreed on the 'identity card' this is then discussed with the learner's line manager and/or HR manager, and agreement is reached on a maximum of three 'soft skills' to be worked on in the coaching. A contract is then drawn up between the learner, the line manager and/or HR manager and the coach.

The next phase is action planning. Here again economies of scale and reduced time are achieved by automating much of the process. The computer produces a suggested learning programme, based on the learner's identity card and on their learning style, and also drawing on Enel's distance learning materials. Some 150 case studies, business games, presentations, reports and so on are available for this e-coaching programme. A key role of the coach is to oversee the selection of appropriate materials and select the best ones for the learner, based on their needs, learning style and preferences. The coach has considerable discretion here and can add to or take away materials suggested through the automated process.

Once the learner agrees the action plan, a timetable is drawn up and the coaching sessions begin. These extend over three months, and the learner is expected to work on the agenda at least once a week and complete the agreed action points. Coach and learner have a one-to-one coaching session on a weekly basis, which mainly takes place through online 'chat': D'Apruzzo has experimented with e-mail but believes this is too stilted and lifeless and does not allow for sufficient 'story-telling'.

As the coaching progresses, the coach can put groups of people with common interests together, or introduce different activities using the webcam, virtual classrooms, discussion groups and so on. This flexibility over learning methods enables the coach to adapt the learning environment to the individual's learning style and preferences. It helps add variety to the learning and also satisfies the need many people have to learn through social interaction.

Throughout this whole process, coach and learner can and, indeed, are generally likely to meet face to face at some time during the coaching.

The first 20 learners had only just completed the programme at the time of publishing this book, and D'Apruzzo is carefully monitoring events. One aspect she is keeping a close eye on is the ratio of learners to coaches, to make sure she has correctly identified the workload. Too many learners for one coach may compromise the quality of the coaching; too few is not cost-efficient. At the moment, she has ten learners to one coach, with one assistant. The role of the assistant is to provide back-up support to the coaches, for instance retrieving materials or perhaps finding new ones to suit a learner's particular requirements. The assistant also acts as a 'help point' for learners – for instance, if they wish to find a particular book, need some information or are having some difficulties. D'Apruzzo does not expect learners will have much difficulty with the technology. This is largely because Enel employees are 'computer-savvy'. D'Apruzzo also believes the technology to be extremely straightforward to use and sufficiently robust for it to be unlikely to cause problems.

D'Apruzzo has appointed high-calibre coaches who have themselves achieved considerable success, either as coaches or in business. In this way, D'Apruzzo ensures that learners will receive the full benefits of one-to-one coaching; this will not just be an online learning exercise with some coaching support.

The e-coaching programme has been set up with automated monitoring and tracking devices so that Sfera can monitor the level of usage without in any way breaking into the confidentiality of what is discussed between coach and learner. One form of monitoring that D'Apruzzo regards as especially significant is to keep track of and analyse which of the group's subsidiary organisations sponsor participants. D'Apruzzo believes the programme is more likely to find favour in businesses with more 'collaborative' and less 'directive' leadership styles, and the programme's 20 initial participants have been carefully chosen from three business units for this reason. D'Apruzzo has built into the system a registration process to capture data about the sponsoring organisation or department, and the culture that prevails there. She has also set up a series of questions for the HR managers of these organisations to enable them to judge how acceptable this e-coaching initiative is likely to be to their organisation.

It has taken D'Apruzzo some 15 months to put this initiative together. Much of this time was taken up translating the idea into an automated product and convincing people who were responsible for different parts of the system, such as the psychologists and training specialists, that their standards and ethics would not be compromised by putting these online. D'Apruzzo certainly believes that Sfera's ability to develop this programme and get as far as it has is thanks to its existing e-learning infrastructure that gave it both the content and the technological platform from which to build this initiative.

The next stage for Sfera and its consultancy partner, Asset Management, to consider is adapting this product for other organisations. Perhaps by finding partners from other countries or industries joint discussion forums and virtual classrooms can extend the horizons for learners, bringing them into contact with other worlds and ways of doing things. This will enrich their skills even further, and may even open additional business opportunities.

KEY LEARNING POINTS

There is much evidence to show that a coach can ensure the success of an e-learning programme.

There are many roles that a coach can carry out in the realm of e-learning. These roles may be performed online or offline. They include building and maintaining the learning community, supporting the learner through the program and monitoring and evaluating usage.

Coaches may work with learners on identifying their needs, selecting suitable programs and materials, helping them with the technology or acting as subject experts who can support and coach where necessary.

Coaches have a crucial role in keeping learners motivated and interested, and in adapting the learning environment to suit their preferred way of learning and to take maximum advantage of the opportunities the online medium offers for social interaction.

Coaches who work in this context need to have the interpersonal and relationship-building skills associated with coaches who perform traditional coaching roles. They also need to have good familiarity with online systems and a range of other skills depending on which of the coaching roles they may perform.

Organisations are beginning to report achieving considerable economies of scale and cost savings through their use of e-learning. This is especially so when e-learning serves a large community and leads to a reduction in the expense and opportunity cost of classroom training. It is also the case when e-learning is developed as a collaborative exercise, where different organisations work together to develop and fund the initiative.

In the case study example of Sfera, we saw that executive coaching can be incorporated into the online learning environment. This too achieves economies of scale and other cost savings. It enables a rich mix of materials to be used and offers considerable flexibility, both to the learner and the organisation. It enables the organisation to keep tighter control over the purpose and content of the coaching. It enables the coach to tailor materials precisely to the individual's requirements. It does require an excellent technological infrastructure, and if online learning materials already exist this will speed up development of the coaching program. It also requires good administrative and organisational skills on the part of the coach to be able to source and tailor materials for each individual learner. The coaching can use a mix of online, face-to-face and telephone methods.

I am convinced that, within the next few years, everyone will use new technology to achieve at least one of their learning goals. Online learning, and with it online coaching, thus has huge potential, which I have scarcely been able to do more than hint at in this chapter.

NOTES AND REFERENCES

1   VAN BUREN M.E. (2002) *State of the Industry: ASTD'S Annual Review of Trends in Employer-Provided training in the United States*. Virginia, American Society for Training and Development.

2   SLOMAN M. *and* ROLF J. (2003) The Change Agenda: e-learning the learning curve. London, CIPD.

3   UK e-learning Survey (2002) ICUS and HR Gateway.com September. www.icus.net.

4   SLOMAN M. *and* ROLF J. (2003) The Change Agenda: e-learning the learning curve. London, CIPD.

5   CHAPMAN B. Comparative Analysis of Enterprise Learning Content Management Systems. California, Brandon-Hall.com

6   SLOMAN. M and TAYLOR J (2002) 'Customising the Learning experience' *Human Resources Decisions International*. London, Sterling Publications. April.

7   DRISCOLL M. Dr (2002) *Web-based Training* (2nd edn). San Fransisco, Jossey-Bass Pfeiffer. April.

Part Two

Managing the coaching process

In Part Two of this book I seek to assist personnel practitioners with the logistics of arranging and managing the coaching process. I put forward ideas on how to work with colleagues to help them choose appropriate learning solutions, identify learning needs, choose an external coach, contract with the coach, manage relationships and evaluate success. I also set out the main skills and techniques of being a coach and look at how HR professionals can themselves use coaching techniques in their day-to-day dealings with their line colleagues. My aim here is to enable HR practitioners to understand the coaching process and manage it.

9

Arranging the coaching

This chapter addresses the question of the role for HR in arranging the coaching and, in doing so, I look at the following questions:

How is a need for coaching identified? What is the process for appointing the coach? How do you set up the coaching relationship? How do you evaluate its success?

IDENTIFYING THE NEED

The first step in arranging coaching must be to identify genuine needs and objectives both for the organisation and the individual. The emphasis is on 'genuine' because the use of coaching has become so widespread in some businesses as to give rise to the criticism that it is merely a fashion accessory: you reach a certain point and demand your coach.

Lucy Kellaway, writing in the *Financial Times* in April 2000 in an article entitled 'Life of a coach potato', caused a storm among executive coaching firms by suggesting that 'having a coach was well on the way to being the biggest status symbol of all'.[1] The extent to which this is actually a problem or, indeed, a bad thing is debatable. If people use coaching as a way of learning and developing and managing change, then maybe it does not matter if they have another agenda as well. It is certainly preferable to feeling one has to hide the fact of seeking support or advice.

My own experience in the HR function of an investment bank included battles to get people in the business areas to accept the usefulness of learning. Most people felt that by the time they had achieved good degrees from Oxford or Cambridge, possibly followed by an accountancy qualification or an MBA, and could, perhaps, point to large fees they had earned for the bank, they already knew everything they needed to know to do their job: the evidence was clear. To find people in a similar role now thinking of coaching as a badge of honour is a remarkable turn-around. The drawback is that while coaching is an enormously powerful tool, success does depend upon the learner truly being committed to it. Using coaching merely as a status symbol implies a lack of focus on genuinely useful objectives.

There are many other inappropriate approaches to coaching that need to be considered, such as employing coaching in political manoeuvring or acquiescing to please others in the organisation. The HR manager of an insurance company reported a situation in his organisation where the MD thinks coaching is a good idea and is sold on the approach used by a particular coaching firm. In the HR manager's opinion, all the coaches do is put people through a psycho-metric test and feed back the results. He does not see any changes in behaviour among the senior management who go through this process, there is no follow-up and, although undoubtedly they set goals, these are not properly defined, linked into the business or backed up by any business process.

There is a considerable onus on all involved, but particularly on the HR manager, to ensure that coaching is arranged appropriately and for the right reasons. This involves focusing on and identifying the genuine needs of the organisation and also of the individual.

Identifying organisational needs

In the first part of this book, I showed how coaching can be a powerful solution to achieving a number of different strategic aims. The case studies reported have a number of things in common, not least the fact that they meet very specific needs and are an integral part of the aims and aspirations of a department or of the organisation and, sometimes, of an entire sector.

The HR manager needs to ensure, initially, that executive coaching really does fit into the overall repertoire of learning and development strategies that are appropriate for both the individual and the organisation. It can be an expensive option if learning needs do not really require this degree of customisation and confidentiality. More importantly, more expensive and exclusive does not automatically mean better – at least not better for everything. Some needs are better served by other approaches – for example, learning in a group of peers.

The HR department should start with the corporate plan for the organisation. From this it should be possible to identify the key people-management requirements and draw up a personnel plan. The issues arising from this plan might range from identifying changes needed to the organisational culture and/or leadership style, to succession planning and future skills requirements. This plan should enable the HR manager to determine the key principles on which coaching for individuals or a coaching programme for a group of individuals would be considered.

A separate set of requirements might be identified for boards of directors, or those at the very top of the organisation. For board directors, the skills once on the board are different from the ones required to reach it. New skills that are required include advocacy, influencing, the ability to present an argument cogently and concisely, and to demonstrate an interest in areas outside one's own discipline. Strategic thinking is often not a vital requirement for roles below the board but is essential for a director.

As well as the relentless demand for bottom-line results, directors' legal and governance responsibilities are growing. The higher directors go up an organisation, the fewer the people in whom they can confide. In the past, for example, the chief executive might have used the chairman or an independent director as a sounding board. But these days many directors feel that it is not wise to open their hearts to the people who determine whether you are the right person for the job, or who may indeed be keen to take your place.

CHAMPIONING COACHING

Even where coaching is accepted within the organisation, there can still be contrary views. Moira Siddons at PwC finds that many managers are reluctant to recommend it for their staff and, similarly, many are reluctant to identify it for themselves. This may be because of competition for funds from other priorities, or because it is often difficult to measure the benefit of coaching. From the line manager's perspective you have to manage your budget and be selective about who uses it. You need to consider the needs of your team and how to prioritise between over- and under-achievers or plateaued performers. People are sometimes hesitant to enter into a coaching relationship – being coached is seen as an unknown area to step into. There is often a low level of clarity around coaching and what it can achieve, and sometimes people confuse it with therapy or fear the risks of disclosure, or see it as remedial and therefore a slur.

For a coaching culture to become embedded it needs champions, the most important being the HR manager. In championing the cause, the HR manager needs to be absolutely clear about what the business objectives are, how coaching can help individuals and the mechanics of how coaching operates. This clear, virtually rehearsed understanding is crucial to being able to answer people's questions convincingly. The HR manager also needs to take every available opportunity to promote the benefits and availability of coaching.

Mark Prime of Citigroup, for example, is regularly asked by a senior line manager for a training course to help someone with management skills. Prime reports that when he looks into the request he often finds that coaching would be a preferable alternative, both for the individual and the organisation. He and his staff spread the word about coaching as much as possible to raise people's awareness of its benefits and to create a positive attitude towards it so that it is seen as developmental and not remedial – and as a possible first option.

As identified in Chapter 12, HR managers need to be able to switch between being internal consultants and internal coaches. Being able to seize the moment and switch into spontaneously coaching a line manager will not only be an effective way of supporting the line manager, it will also provide the proof that coaching works.

IDENTIFYING INDIVIDUAL NEEDS

Having set the parameters for coaching in the organisation and created some fertile ground, there are four ways of identifying the individual's learning needs:

The individuals identify these themselves

This might come about through 360-degree feedback. This is now a valuable and regularly used tool that has done a great deal to help successful and less successful people recognise areas for development.

The need is identified by the learner's manager

The most usual time for identifying learning needs is during performance appraisal, or through the manager's day-to-day observation of the learner, especially when there are some changes occurring in the workplace that affect the learner.

The need is identified by a third party

This may arise from the HR department or a more senior manager, or even a peer of the individual.

The coaching is linked to a training programme.

SETTING UP AND MANAGING THE COACHING RELATIONSHIP

Many HR people find it helpful to have a set procedure for setting up coaching relationships for individuals. Neil Hoskings describes formal procedures he previously instigated at an American bank where executive coaching was frequently used:

1 The HR manager and the line manager identify the issue and any barriers or particular difficulties.

2 The line manager positions this with team members.

3 HR discusses with the individual/s and 'tests the issue'. For example, 'What is your perception?' 'What did you agree with your line manager?'

4 If there are discrepancies then the HR manager has a further discussion with the line manager.

5 When the HR manager is comfortable that both parties have a clear understanding of the issue, the HR manager then needs to get an idea of the type of coach the learner would most like to work with. (Note: using Witherspoon's continuum of coaching roles may be helpful here.) The HR manager also needs to get an idea of the type of personality and background the learner is likely to get on with best and respect.

6 The HR manager then introduces two or three coaches to the learner.

7 The learner selects a coach, who submits a proposal based on a preliminary identification of needs, and the HR manager negotiates a contract with the coach.

8 The coaching is evaluated, and the learner and the coach prepare feedback reports.

Hoskings has developed extensive coaching guidelines for learners and line managers to help them understand the coaching process. He has also developed a coaching database containing basic information, such as the names of the coaches, their areas of speciality, contact details, and experience of organisation and industry. It is a secure database, as it contains sensitive information.

MANAGING THE EXPECTATIONS OF THE LINE MANAGER

These coaching procedures require careful and judicious management, not least when it comes to managing the expectations of the line manager and determining the line manager's role in the coaching relationship. Coaches need wide latitude to work with 'the whole person' and help each learner be more effective as a person as well as to be more effective as a business leader. The line manager is one of the parties, albeit a 'passive' one, to the coaching, and it is up to the HR manager to ensure they understand their role and how to manage it.

The HR manager needs to ensure:

- They are specific about the business results they want.

- They negotiate these with the learners.

- They have set aside the budget required.

- They sanction the learner's time availability.

- They do not expect to get information back on the person, neither will they ask for this.

- They do not change the goal posts during the process; or, if they do, they handle it sensitively, explaining the reasons.

- They will discuss with the learner what they feel they gained from the coaching, so as to ascertain whether it was worthwhile and for guidance on arranging any future coaching relationships.

- They do not put unrealistic pressures on the employee, such as: 'We are spending money on you – why aren't you doing it?'

- They hold back from influencing the employee on what coaching or which coach to choose.

Assisting the individual learner

Support from either the line manager or the HR manager is essential to help the individual learner identify their needs, select a coach and get the best out of the coaching relationship.

It is therefore worth examining in detail how the HR manager and the line manager can support the learner.

Is coaching the right solution?

A first task is to make sure coaching is the right solution for this particular learner. Some people may not respond well to coaching, for instance, if they:

- *are not willing to make the effort to change:* this may arise because they do not see the need to change, or because they feel coaching is a punishment or a manifestation of failure. They may not trust their line manager's motives and fear the line manager is seeking feedback on them to show they are not performing.

  Signs to watch out for are if the learner is defensive and seeks others to blame, or denies the impact of their behaviour, or seems unwilling to tackle options because they 'have tried it already and it doesn't work'. Other signs may be that the individual appears embarrassed about being coached and does not wish others to know about it.

  Creating an understanding that coaching is positive and developmental may help here, but otherwise it is likely to require time and patience on the part of the HR manager, using a coaching style, to turn an unwilling person around. Whether it is worth giving this responsibility to the coach will depend on a host of circumstances, not least the time and budget available.

- *have unrealistic expectations:* this is where the learner thinks that coaching is a quick-fix solution and does not fully understand that it takes time and effort to change behaviour. (See also: Is the learner ready for coaching? Chapter 11, page 147).

- *have been 'written off' by the company:* in these circumstances, it may be more helpful to arrange outplacement counselling, or move the person to a more suitable role.

- *are in the wrong job:* again, it may be more appropriate to move the person to a more suitable role.

How to match learner and coach

Having identified whether coaching is the right solution for the person, the next stage is to identify a suitable coach. Witherspoon's continuum of coaching roles can assist here in helping the HR manager focus the discussion with the learner in order to identify a suitable coach and draw up contract terms.

- *Coaching for skills:* where the learner needs quick help to learn a skill. The coach needs to be an expert in the field, and the coaching is likely to be completed in a short time span.

- *Coaching for performance:* where the coaching is to focus on the learner's performance in their current role. Such coaching is often appropriate for managers facing difficult obstacles, taking on new responsibilities, or where organisational change is fast-paced. The HR manager may be helpful here in assisting the learner assemble diagnostic data. Performance coaches may need to have expertise in the arena of choice, or be able to introduce someone with specific skills, if required.

- *Coaching for development:* this is where the aim is to support the individual's career or role development or help them identify career options. Again the HR manager can help the learner collect diagnostic data. The HR manager's role may also be able to provide career information. Coaches may need to be specialists in career development, or may have more generalist backgrounds.

- *Coaching to the executive's agenda:* this is the most open-ended of all the coaching roles. The HR manager needs to obtain as good an idea as possible of the type of personality, approach and background that will best suit the learner so as to effect a good match. The HR manager needs to decide whether the coach must be a subject expert. It is likely that the coach will be required to have access to people who are, and the coach often needs to be of a similar level and status to the person being coached.

A question that HR practitioners frequently have to address when arranging executive agenda coaching is the extent to which the learner also requires a coach who can look at personal problems. Perhaps these problems are impinging on the individual at work?

Bob Garratt, an executive coach who works at board level, frequently finds that a learner has worries outside work that can be easily dealt with. These may have been troubling the individual for some time, such as knowing you need to draw up your will but never quite getting round to it. Or perhaps the learner realises he needs to change his behaviour in some way, but this is deep-rooted, requiring a more intensive executive agenda coaching.

Siddons at PwC believes that:

> *one of the most important elements of successful coaching is the depth at which the learner is prepared to work. The deeper and more psychological this is, the more real and sustained any changes within the individual. Most of the business coaches that work with or for PwC are also trained counsellors and/or psychologists, enabling the learner to make safe choices about the depth of personal work that they are willing to take on. This has significant advantages both for the business and for the individuals.*

Myles Downey, Director of Studies at the School of Coaching, believes that coaches need a clear understanding of their role as a coach and must be able to identify when there are issues that could benefit from a therapeutic intervention that is beyond their role and responsibility and, often, competence and experience as a coach. In his view, however, coaching demands its own skill set which is 'neither a psychologist, nor psycotherapist, nor sports-based'.[2]

As a buyer of coaching services Prime believes 'it has to be the business need first'. He sees coaching as a business methodology and seeks to identify how the coaching will help the business. He also prefers to appoint coaches who have appropriate business backgrounds so that they can better understand the pressures executives have to face.

Hoskings also puts business needs first and makes the point that a good interaction from an employee's point of view can be quite different from one the organisation sees as good.

The US coach and clinical psychologist Steven Berglas, writing in the *Harvard Business Review,*[3] has raised an interesting and controversial issue. He reasoned that an unqualified coach may do more harm than good if the person he or she is coaching has a psychological disorder. To protect against this, Berglas suggested that everyone should receive a psychological evaluation before coaching commences. 'By screening out employees not psychologically prepared or predisposed to benefit from the process, companies avoid putting executives in deeply uncomfortable – even damaging – positions.' Berglas also suggests that 'companies should hire independent mental health professionals to review coaching outcomes. This helps to ensure that coaches are not ignoring underlying problems or creating new ones.'

Prime, putting across the line manager's point of view, concurs with this approach and sees it as 'important to distinguish between therapy that an occupational health department should get involved in and coaching for business performance'. However, he concedes that 'there is a grey area here that needs careful consideration to avoid possible damaging implications'.

Professor Cary Cooper, BUPA Professor of Organisational Psychology at UMIST, is of the view that if the executive is primarily concerned with developing their career or striking a better work–life balance, a mental health approach is unnecessary. 'But, if an individual has lots of personal problems that are holding them back at work, then they probably need a coach who has a background in psychology.'

Others take the view that a psychologist or psychotherapist can do more harm than good when coaching, by trying to dig things up for people unnecessarily. As one executive coach said to me: 'It is important to keep a sense of perspective and bear in mind that many of us are healthily neurotic and that the most amenable of us can have relationships that go wrong. This does not mean we need psychological assessments and help to put us right.'

In summary, I would say that some understanding of psychology at work is necessary for the coach to be able to administer psychometric or other diagnostic instruments, to be able to give feedback and understand how people react. In all coaching circumstances, it is important for the coach to know the boundaries within which they can operate and know when to refer someone for counselling or psychotherapy.

The HR manager, in presenting a shortlist to the learner, might include someone with a psychotherapy background and someone with a different type of background to help the learner to make the decision. There may be some cases where the HR manager may judge that an individual is most likely to require a psychological or psychotherapy approach – for instance, if the individual is known as a bully.

If the coach is to work with a senior-ranking executive, then it is important to ascertain from the executive if they prefer a coach who has worked at that level so that coach and learner can have sensible conversations about business strategy and organisational development.

Mike Laws at Ernst & Young knows his colleagues well, and this enables him to assess the type of person they may most respect. He also has extensive discussions with his colleagues to identify their preferences – for example, if they want someone who has managed a business or been involved in a merger.

Hoskings puts forward a slightly different viewpoint. He feels the coach's background is not relevant to success. It is how they use the skills they have and how they relate to people and get into a relationship. This is better than what is in the kit bag.

CRITERIA FOR APPOINTING A COACH

It is helpful to identify the criteria against which you will select a coach. The following are some of the points to consider, along with the views of the HR managers I interviewed:

- *Training and qualifications:* what training and/or qualifications does the coach have and are they relevant? What evidence is there of continuing professional development?

  The HR managers I contacted expressed a universal preference for coaches to have at their disposal a range of tools, especially diagnostics. They do not rate coaches who use tools for the sake of using them, or who dogmatically use just one model, around which they enthusiastically base all their coaching. Rather, they like to see a range of tools to show the coach is able to be flexible towards the needs of the learner.

They prefer coaches to be good process people who can structure not just a session but the whole coaching programme. One HR manager recalled a coach who said, 'I have the experience, I can talk.' HR managers require a better definition of the route the coach proposes using.

Most HR managers look for evidence that the coach is aware of the boundaries of the coaching relationship and that they are able to cope if the coaching uncovers something unexpected.

- *Experience:* some HR managers look for business focus. Others believe this is unnecessary and may even prefer the coach to have a completely different background so as to offer a broader perspective to the learner.

  HR managers often expect coaches to have their own life experience and context to draw on, not because they want them to have 'answers' but because they feel that they are then better placed to relate to the learner and find things in common.

  One HR manager places importance on the people the coach generally works with so as to gauge the kind of experience they have gained. Some people say they only coach board directors, which clearly limits their range. Most coaches quote details of their successes and turnover. One HR manager prefers to find out about the length of their coaching relationships and whether they obtain repeat assignments from their client organisations.

  Many HR managers seek a diversity in their pool of coaches by age, gender and so on, believing this allows more chance of finding an appropriate and congenial match with their different learners.

- *Style, chemistry and behavioural competencies:* can the coach demonstrate good active listening skills? Can they maintain strict confidentiality? Can they enable people to set objectives that explore new horizons? Can they see programmes through? Do they fit with the culture and style of the organisation and of the learner? What is their own level of self-awareness? Why are they working as a coach? Is it to help themselves, or to help others? Do they have the ability to challenge learners? Do they inspire trust and motivation?

- *Measuring success:* what indication can they give of how the coaching programme will be measured? How do they measure their own success? Do they receive coaching, or some other form of supervision?

The HR manager should provide prospective coaching clients with information about the coaches, including their education and coaching credentials, functional expertise, business experience and other background information.

THE RELATIONSHIP BETWEEN HR AND THE COACH

Many HR managers find it beneficial to maintain regular relationships with coaches and meet up with them frequently, even if there is no current assignment. Coaches are more effective when they can identify with and talk about the realities of the learner's working environment. This is more easily achieved if the HR manager is prepared to give the coach a grounding in the business and culture of the organisation. The HR manager should keep the coach updated on changes and inform the coach about the development interventions that are available internally, about relevant internal relationships and about major change initiatives.

Confidentiality between coach and learner is vital, but many HR managers expect coaches who work with a number of people in the organisation to give them feedback about any issues that seem to crop up regularly.

Should you use an internal or an external coach?

Many organisations use internal coaches or mentors. We saw the examples of KPMG and Lloyds TSB, where internal coaches are used for career development coaching. These same organisations, as is common with so many others, use internal people (usually known as mentors) to support a more junior colleague, to help them get to know the organisation or to help them with their career development. One learner describes the advantages of having an internal coach or mentor:

> It can raise awareness of your abilities and give you a broader understanding of the organisation and why it chooses certain strategies. It can give you insights into organisational decision-making and can certainly help you understand other roles and activities. Very importantly, having the sponsorship of someone in the organisation can really help your career.

The HR manager has a useful role in keeping a database of internal mentors and coaches, and in facilitating networking activities or other ways in which internal coaches can support one another. Examples of these were given in the case studies in Part One.

Ensuring confidentiality and professionalism is just as crucial with internal coaches as with external ones. It sometimes requires a more delicate balancing act. One career coach described the following dilemma she once faced. She was told by a learner in a coaching session that he felt undervalued and feared he did not have a future in the organisation. The coach, however, knew this person was considered to be a high-flier, but she resisted the temptation of telling him so. She also resisted the temptation of rushing to his line manager to say, 'Look, you must do something about so and so.' Instead, she successfully coached the learner to discuss the matter with his line manager. In this way, she maintained the confidentiality and impartiality of the relationship.

There are many instances when it is best to use an external coach who can bring an unbiased and fresh view on problems and who also has views and knowledge gained from working with other organisations. People can stretch and expand with the right coach, whether it be an internal or external one, but many issues are best discussed with an objective third party. Examples might be when you are thinking of reorganising or want to know how to deal with an individual with whom you have a personality clash.

One of the main values of a coach is to have someone who holds an objective perspective and who has no baggage or investment in the outcome. It can be difficult for an internal coach to achieve this or to be perceived in this impartial way.

THE CONTRACT

A formal contract should always be drawn up, setting out the parameters and logistics of the relationship and also identifying the different parties and the role of each. This sets expectations and clarifies administrative matters.

The following section outlines some of the points that should be included in the contract and some of the issues that need to be considered.

1 The parties to the contract and their roles

There are essentially three parties to the contract: the learner, the organisation and the coach. This is complicated by the fact that the organisation is not monolithic: it may be represented by the HR department and the learner's line manager. There may also be other individuals or departments taking an informal interest. For example, the chief executive may take an interest in the development of a senior manager with identified potential.

2 Objectives of the relationship

There are three broad objectives of the contract:

- to facilitate the executive's learning
- to facilitate the organisation's learning
- to achieve identified business results.

HR has an extremely important role to play in facilitating the smooth running of the coaching relationship by:

- ensuring all parties are clear and specific about the desired business results
- managing the organisation's expectations
- managing the individual's expectations
- managing feedback.

HR also needs to ensure that the learner and the line manager have reasonable expectations about the coaching. There needs to be a clear understanding between the person who authorises the funding and the coach about the aims of the coaching and how many sessions are approved. Specifying objectives and other matters in this way ensures that it will be clear when the coaching is finished, thus avoiding the learner becoming dependent on the coach.

Many people wish to discuss career issues during the course of coaching. It is wise to discuss this eventuality at the time of drawing up the contract and to specify whether or not the coach has permission to provide career coaching.

3 Pre-coaching meeting, assessment and data-gathering

The coach and learner should meet at least once to set out and agree the logistics of the arrangement. This follows after an initial meeting or meetings, which are part of the engagement process: it is not appropriate to discuss arrangements in detail until the appointment has been agreed.

Here again HR may be able to play a role by providing background information about the executive and the organisation.

If the coaching is to be carried out by telephone, it may be logistically difficult for coach and learner to meet. Many telephone coaches offer a free, trial telephone session to enable the learner to decide whether theirs is an approach that suits.

The contract should specify what information will be used and what other instruments the coach will use for gathering data.

4 Development plan

The contract should state roughly when the goals will be set for the coaching. This should be as soon as possible after the preparatory data-gathering and feedback. The individual's personal learning goals should be kept confidential between coach and learner but the business goals should be confirmed to HR and the learner's line manager. I recommend identifying no more than four business goals, otherwise the coaching is likely to lose focus and only the more easily attainable goals will be achieved.

5 Timing, frequency, duration and location of coaching sessions

The contract should specify the time, place and duration of coaching sessions, while also allowing reasonable flexibility on both sides.

Coaches have differing views as to the appropriate length of a coaching session. Some prefer a brisk approach, and their sessions rarely last longer than an hour. Others, especially when clients are flying in from overseas, run half-day or one-day sessions. Some points to bear in mind are that coaching can be intense, and an hour might well be as much as a learner can take, especially if they are required to consider 'difficult' or 'unwelcome' issues. There are also some situations where learners need to work in a sustained fashion on issues that require a lot of thinking through, and these may require a longer session. On the other hand, some sessions may be more action-based and the coaching may be much shorter.

The total duration and frequency of a coaching assignment will also vary considerably depending on the aims of the coaching. Executive agenda coaching relationships, in particular, often last for as long as one year or more. Mentoring relationships and internal skills coaching may continue indefinitely. Especially with performance coaching, between four and eight sessions is often sufficient. As regards frequency, I find two-weekly intervals work best, as it leaves people time to reflect as well as to do any work or reading. I often also allow a three- or even four-week gap in the middle, again to allow adequate reflection.

Most coaches who are providing telephone coaching fix times and dates with their learners for the session, and each learner calls them, rather than the other way around. This psychologically helps the learner prepare and get ready for the session, which they may be less inclined to do if they wait to be called.

Many telephone coaching assignments are arranged so that coach and learner meet up at some stage. This might be at the initial stage, to go through feedback and set up the coaching plan. Sometimes it is at certain points of the coaching where coach and learner need to hold longer, more exploratory sessions.

The contract should include a notice period and payment for termination in the event that the relationship is not working or that business factors interfere with its continuation. Clearly, this must be two-sided, also allowing the coach to withdraw.

6 Confidentiality

Confidentiality is absolutely vital to protect trust and to create a safe environment in which learners feel free to discuss fears and difficulties and examine risky options. The contract must spell this out explicitly, so that there cannot be any misunderstanding of what may have been expected. This goes beyond discussing what passes in meetings with the learner but also concerns recording, filing and accessing any data or notes of meetings. The contract will also commit the coach to maintain confidentiality regarding information on the organisation or its competitors that may be commercially sensitive. It is appropriate for the coach to acknowledge in the contract that, in the course of their work, they may become aware of 'price-sensitive information' in relation to publicly quoted companies. They must undertake not to reveal or to use this.

As a corollary, they should usually undertake not to approach employees of the organisation for commercial purposes either during or after the coaching assignment.

Clarifications about any intellectual property rights may also need to be made.

The organisation should not expect any feedback from the coach except in the limited circumstances outlined below under 'feedback' and evaluation.

If the coach collects information on the learner from other people, the coach must make it clear how the information will be used and fed back. For example, the coach may feed back to the learner verbatim comments from colleagues without identifying who made them. It is important to maintain this anonymity scrupulously.

7 Feedback and evaluation

Feedback arrangements need to be agreed between all parties and specified in the contract. The objectives of feedback are:

- to be able to address any problems arising between learner and coach
- to be able to amend targets if appropriate
- to identify what is and isn't working and to choose appropriate techniques.

The learner should be prepared to give the coach regular and honest feedback.

If someone is coaching several people in the same organisation, then the coach may agree to feed back common issues to the organisation without identifying individuals and only with their agreement. This can be enormously helpful to the organisation in addressing problems it may not have been aware of.

The contract should specify how the coaching will be evaluated.

8 Payment and frequency of payment

Fees, the basis of calculation of any extra payments, and when they will be invoiced should be specified in the contract. The organisation should commit to paying invoices promptly and within the payment deadlines requested.

Some coaches expect their clients to pay in advance after they have been selected from any shortlist. As small, independent businesses they are not in a position to deal with the extended payment terms companies often apply to suppliers.

Billable expenses should also be agreed, even if this is kept as vague as 'necessary expenses will be invoiced at cost on the basis of receipts submitted'. It is as well to agree in advance if, for instance, travel expenses will be invoiced.

9 External resources

It is useful to specify what skills the coach will or, more importantly, will not bring to the relationship. If external experts may be required for specific skills training, financial expertise, etc then the contract should make it clear that these will be arranged by agreement. This avoids any later disagreement over what the coach undertook to provide.

In setting up the contract the learner needs also to consider what the organisation will contribute to the development plan. They need to go back to the organisation and say, 'I have done this but you need to do these things.'

How much should the coaching cost?

Coaching is a relatively expensive option because coaches will often have to charge a full day's fee for what may be only a couple of hours' work. They can rarely simply leave one assignment and turn on a tap of other fee-paying work for the rest of the day. Most coaches will be flexible. If you use a coach regularly, it may be advantageous to both parties if you pay them a retainer. This would cover a specified number of hours of coaching a year.

Telephone coaching generally works out more cost-effective for the client, as you pay only for the focused coaching and not for any travelling or other time. The coach may benefit from this too by being able to take on more assignments in the time they might otherwise have spent travelling. Mike Travis, a US-based executive coach who coaches almost exclusively by telephone, generally has around 60 to 70 learners a year.

EVALUATION

One of the 'hot topics' of HR management is how to evaluate learning. It hardly needs saying that if coaching does not achieve benefits that are worth more than its cost to the organisation then it is irrational to pursue it. Indeed, a sensible manager will be seeking a significant margin of benefit over cost, to allow for errors in identifying and allocating costs.

In skills coaching, it is often possible to set quantifiable objectives. For instance, if the goal is to improve an individual's presentation skills or their public speaking, then it is usually clear to the individual and their listeners whether this has happened. The problem of evaluating coaching arises when the goals are more ambitious and more complex.

For example, suppose an objective is to achieve a better strategic outlook. The business area the learner leads subsequently performs poorly: is this an indication of an unsuccessful programme? Not necessarily: the learning may have led to better decisions, but that does not guarantee improved business performance. Long-established problems may have overwhelmed the improvements.

Following on from this, we must recognise that the outcome of coaching initiatives is intrinsically bound up with what else is going on in the organisation. Therefore any measurement of effectiveness must make an effort to isolate the outcomes of coaching from these extraneous factors. To illustrate this, suppose an individual's performance is potentially improved through coaching, but shifting responsibilities within the organisation frustrates their actual performance. This is neither the fault of the individual nor of the coaching.

Let us consider the four levels of training evaluation first identified by Dr Donald Kirkpatrick in 1959.[4] Kirkpatrick's thesis is still widely regarded as the most authoritative in the field. The Investors in People standard uses it as a framework, as does the CIPD's *'Making Training Pay'* material. Although Kirkpatrick was looking specifically at training, his thesis applies to all forms of learning, including coaching:

- *Reaction:* what does the learner feel about the learning event?
- *Learning:* what facts, knowledge, etc did the learner gain?
- *Behaviours:* what skills did the learner develop, ie what new information is the learner using on the job?
- *Results or effectiveness:* what results occurred, ie did the learner apply the new skills to the necessary tasks in the organisation and, if so, what results were achieved?

Although the fourth level, evaluating results and effectiveness, is the most desired result from learning, it is usually the most difficult to accomplish for two reasons. The first is the difficulty of accurate measurement. Evaluating effectiveness often involves the use of key performance measures, eg faster and more reliable output from the machine after the operator has been trained, higher ratings on employee opinion surveys from the trained supervisor, etc. But these measures may be highly subjective and only capable of measuring at second or even third hand, by looking at the effects that result from achieving the objective.

The second problem is that evaluation is time-consuming and, therefore, expensive for all concerned. It is particularly because of this latter problem that evaluation does not happen. Finding the time is, in most cases, a bigger barrier than knowing 'how' to do the evaluation. Is it time well spent to go back to learners some time after the event or to contact their managers, peers and customers to collect information through interviews and questionnaires? I would say that it is hugely expensive of the time of everyone who is diverted from their normal work to do so. Further, one could argue that learning is an indisputably good thing and that if the learner, the coach and the line manager form a consensus that it has worked, then it has. I would not argue that there should be no attempt made to see whether coaching is working, merely that a sense of proportion should be applied to the amount of effort expended.

Let us consider in more detail Kirkpatrick's four levels.

First, what do we evaluate? Are we evaluating all the coaching carried out in the organisation, a particular coaching initiative, the individual coaches, the learners, or the HR department or person who arranged the coaching?

Continuing the example given above, if we could demonstrate that an individual has not become a more strategic manager as a result of coaching, which of the many possible causes listed above is or are the culprits, and what would we do about it? Of course, this does presuppose that we are sure that the individual's skills really haven't improved. Suppose that they make one important and brilliant decision subsequent to the coaching. Did coaching cause the decision, or would it have been made anyway? We will never know, but it could have justified a lifetime of coaching and many times the actual expense.

Another issue of measurement is that it is frequently pointless to ask 'What business results were achieved as a result of coaching?', because the goal of coaching may be one of preventing mistakes, errors, defects and waste, rather than correcting them. As is the case with training, it is sometimes the case with coaching that the true measure of its value lies in the cost of its absence rather than the benefit of its presence.

So, we have seen there is a problem of knowing what exactly to evaluate. The next issue is what to do with the results of formal, structured and expensive after-the-fact evaluations. What would you do, for instance, if you commissioned a formal evaluation and it revealed that the money you spent on coaching was wasted? Do you know why it has not worked? Can you correct the defects? Would coaching be cost-effective if you could correct the defects?

Suddenly, having got an answer to what seemed to be a key question, one finds they are only the foothills of a whole mountain range of questions which are even more costly and time-consuming to resolve. Of course, it is better to know that it is not working so that it can be dealt with, rather than continuing to pour money into a black hole. I am not suggesting you shirk the issue, but I am suggesting that you consider these facts carefully before undertaking an evaluation.

Another issue relates to the concept of value. To evaluate coaching is to determine its value. But value can be relative, depending upon individual perception. What is of great value to one person is of little or no value to another. In evaluating coaching, then, it is important to know 'from whose point of view'. As noted earlier, there are several possible audiences for evaluation results, including: the learners, their managers, the coaches and their managers, and the executives of the organisation where the coaching is taking place. For example, if someone becomes a more pleasant colleague as a result of coaching, that may mean nothing to one possible evaluator but be hugely worthwhile to another.

Because the definition and perception of value varies from person to person, so do the purposes of evaluation. Moreover, the various audiences for evaluation frequently act as their own evaluators.

In summary, to evaluate coaching properly requires thinking through the purposes of the coaching, the purposes of the evaluation, the audiences for the evaluation results, the time perspective to be employed, and what one might do with the results.

A pragmatic approach to evaluation

In the light of what has been discussed above, I recommend developing a measurement capability that requires an organisational view and a strategic approach to the provision of coaching. I advocate a pragmatic approach to evaluating individual assignments that is generally subjective.

Many of the HR managers I met who are responsible for coaching put the effort in up-front to identify whether coaching is the optimum solution and what it should achieve, leaving the analysis of whether it was worthwhile to the learner, their manager and the coach. Most HR managers take the view that if the coach is 'wrong' or if coaching turns out to be ineffective, they will hear about it. A number of HR managers believe that if the time-conscious, highly demanding learners of their organisation see the coaching through and have not come storming in complaining, this can be taken as evidence that the coaching is effective and worthwhile.

Many of the organisations featured in this book are aiming, through their culture and their people-processes, to get people to see that the way they manage relationships and manage staff directly affects the bottom line. This maintains the emphasis on profitability but alters perceptions of the way to get there.

As we saw in the examples of the BBC, KPMG and Ernst & Young, these organisations consistently promote their core values through value statements and behavioural indicators that then feed into programmes such as 360-degree feedback, employee surveys, and training and development initiatives.

The following are examples of indicators that can be used in opinion surveys to help determine the overall effectiveness to the organisation of coaching and other people-oriented exercises:

- 'I receive regular and timely feedback and coaching from my manager'
- 'My manager encourages me to develop my skills and knowledge'
- 'On my team, we regularly exchange ideas and opinions'
- 'On my team we seek others' opinions before making a decision'
- 'My manager listens, questions and seeks feedback from me before making a decision'
- 'I have had a career development discussion in the past six months'
- 'I have a personal development plan'
- 'I receive regular and valuable feedback and coaching'.

Some organisations are using the balanced scorecard method of measuring the business. This is a way of maintaining the emphasis on the bottom line but also ensures that stakeholders measure success through other, non-financial indicators. Examples of some of the people-measures used on a balanced scorecard are:

- all staff have a personal development plan and career review plan
- scores on employee surveys or 360-feedback
- numbers promoted, moved laterally or who have been trained, or who have enlarged their jobs
- achievement of objectives set for training or for coaching
- productivity v profitabiity ratios
- anecdotal evidence
- values surveys or ethics surveys
- diversity measures
- management of poor and high performance

Feedback for HR

Many HR managers seek anecdotal evidence at the end of a coaching assignment, or ask if the learner recommends their coach to others and on what basis. The value in doing this is to build up understanding of the coach and the type of learner they are best matched with. In addition, this approach measures the effectiveness of coaching, albeit at second hand, through the level of demand.

Feedback for the line manager

Line managers need to identify at the outset the business needs that coaching is to meet and then make some kind of a judgement as to whether the needs were met and the extent to which the coaching contributed. There are several ways of doing this.

Sometimes, evaluation is made against quantifiable measures, such as in the example in Chapter 4 of coaching in call centres.

Often, there is no formal evaluation conducted, rather it is intuitive: the learners and their line managers 'know' that skills are improving and individuals are credited for the improvement in their performance appraisal.

In one organisation where I have coached, the learners submitted feedback reports to the MD, who was their line manager. This had the added benefit of bringing the MD into the loop and giving him an understanding of what had been learned, so that he could support the individuals and allow them to do things differently. Many learners will not go to the trouble of writing a report, but they should be encouraged to discuss their learning with their line mangers so that the line manager can assess the value of the coaching and understand what has been gained.

Quite often measurement involves 'before' and 'after' analyses, usually through 360-degree feedback.

Feedback for the coaches themselves

It is invaluable for a coach to obtain feedback which they can learn from and which will help them improve their effectiveness.

Ideally, coaches should seek feedback from the learner at different stages through the coaching. At which stage this is appropriate will depend upon how long the coaching programme is intended to continue. I believe it is appropriate to expect to see some improvement and change in behaviour after about three sessions, and the coach should be asking the learner what changes they have noticed in their behaviours, attitude to work, relationship with fellow workers, job satisfaction and so on.

Certainly, all coaches should have ways of evaluating their own performance. This may be by seeking feedback from their learners, by looking critically at how they handled things, and by themselves having a coach and being coached on how they handled things, without revealing confidences.

Some coaches determine their own success by whether the key deliverables agreed at the start of the coaching are achieved. They also measure success according to whether the client organisation offers them further work and is prepared to recommend the coach to others.

Most coaches regularly ask their learners for feedback at different stages of the assignment, and stress that if the learner is not happy they should discuss this with their HR manager.

Some coaches carry out evaluations at later stages, contacting the learner to see what progress occurred. It is the coach who stands to gain most from evaluating coaching in this way.

Marketing coaching in the organisation

It is hard to deny the assertion that no organisation should pour money into coaching unless it is working. It therefore seems reasonable to insist that the HR department measures this.

I have argued that it is hard to decide what to measure and why, and that even then the cost of evaluation can be both high and disproportionate to the benefit. The emphasis on formal evaluation of coaching falls into the trap of seeing a particular issue in isolation. By analogy there are many specific jobs undertaken by a marketing or accounting department whose worth is hard to assess in isolation, yet they form part of the larger picture of what those activities do. Similarly, the HR department is charged with improving the quality of management processes, which, if successful in total, undeniably improve the effectiveness of the organisation.

The task of the HR department is more a case of persuading senior management that learning initiatives undertaken to date justify yet more of the same initiative or another, different but related initiative. The inevitable conclusion is that the key issue of evaluation is not one of measurement but of marketing.

A marketing-based approach would propose that:

- Managers' abilities to manage relationships as well as to recruit, motivate and develop their staff are as important as their technical abilities.
- All staff need to be constantly developing their knowledge and improving their

interpersonal, management and technical skills in order to keep the business moving ahead.

- Everyone needs to be able to share ideas and knowledge in order to keep the business moving ahead.

- Everyone needs time to reflect on their experiences and their learning.

- People need to support one another and seek support to promote their development.

- People, by and large, have potential for self-improvement and hence for improved performance.

These key propositions should be included consistently in the organisation's practices and processes so that everyone is consciously and unconsciously aware of them.

In almost all the examples of successful coaching initiatives given in this book, we have seen that HR managers choose champions to be the first to try an initiative and then to help spread and promote it throughout the organisation. We have seen that many of these initiatives are backed up by dedicated intranet sites that promote and inform. They include statistics and concrete and anecdotal evidence about what learning has been carried out and what it has achieved. These are undeniably the badges of a public relations or marketing approach.

KEY LEARNING POINTS

This chapter has taken a wide-ranging view of the role of the HR manager in managing the coaching process. Key responsibilities can be summed up as follows:

- Spread the word subtly and also explicitly in the organisation of what coaching is and its benefits.

- Spot opportunities (working in partnership with the business) where coaching is a solution to a strategic issue and is the right learning solution for certain individuals.

- Be clear about the different types of coaching there are and help individuals decide which type of coaching will suit them.

- Understand diagnostic tools, and know and understand those currently used in the organisation (for example, if there is a 360-process based on the organisation's competency profile, or if the organisation uses particular psychometric instruments on a leadership or team development programme).

- Build a network of coaches and develop a relationship with them.

- Keep these coaches informed about the organisation as much as possible so that the coaches understand the culture, the values, the aims and the activities of the organisation.

- Know how to match coach with learner.

- Set up contractual arrangements with coaches, including fee levels and payment processes.

- Ensure feedback mechanisms are in place so that learner feeds back to coach, to HR and to line manager.

- Establish evaluation of individual and overall coaching programmes.

- Manage the expectations of learner and line manager.

- Market the key people-management propositions throughout the organisation.

NOTES AND REFERENCES

1   KELLAWAY L. (2000) 'The life of a coach potato' *Financial Times*. 14 February.

2   CRIBBS G. (2002) 'The perils of choosing the right business coach' *Financial Times*. 2 December.

3   SIMMS J. (2002) 'Guiding stars' *Director Magazine*. October.

4   BERGLAS S. (2002) 'The very real dangers of executive coaching' *Harvard Business Review*. June.

5   KIRKPATRICK D. (1998) *Another Look at Evaluating Training Programs*. Virginia, American Society for Training and Development.

    This book is a compilation of all evaluation articles published from 1987 to 1988 in *Training and Development*. Dr Donald Kirkpatrick deems these fifty articles 'best practices'.

10

The view from the coach

The primary focus throughout this book has been on what coaching enables a learner to do and an organisation to achieve. This chapter shifts the perspective a little to look at coaching from the coach's point of view. What does a coach do in a session? How do they do it and what do they need to know? What of coaching by telephone or online: do these require different skills?

I hope the discussion of these issues will give HR professionals additional insights that will enable them to manage the coaching process better, promote coaching in the organisation and identify when it is an appropriate learning solution. I hope, especially, that the models, processes and competencies identified here will assist HR professionals in developing their own roles as HR coaches.

WHAT DOES COACHING ENTAIL?
The coaching model

This book is based on a model where a coach is a collaborative partner who works with the learner to help them achieve goals, solve problems, learn and develop. This contrasts with the prevalent model of coaching a decade ago, where coaching was primarily remedial and emphasised where performance and behaviour were unsatisfactory, and the coaching style was usually directive.

Perry Zeus and Dr Suzanne Skiffington have set out an essential difference between the traditional and new models of coaching: 'In the old coaching model employees have difficulties in functioning and don't know why. In the new coaching model, employees are already successful and eager to move to a higher level of functioning but don't know how.' [1]

The new model is a conversation, with the coach asking pertinent questions at critical junctures and encouraging the learner to look at their situation from different angles and explore alternative strategies. There are many different forms of coaching conversation. They range from 'spontaneous coaching', which addresses a short, specific matter, to ongoing, structured sessions to guide and support long-lasting change on the part of the learner. If coaching is to be effective, all of these conversations need to follow a clear process. This does not exclude variation in detail to suit circumstances and personalities, but there needs to be a broad structure that does not change. In Chapter 2, I set out such a process when coaching spontaneously that I call the

'SNIP model'. The following process is one that applies to all structured forms of coaching, whether with individuals or with teams.

A process for the coaching session

- review of action points from last session and reflecting on the learning
- setting goals for this session
- working through the goals and identifying options and solutions
- reflecting on the learning from this session and setting action points to be worked on between this and the next session.

Coaches need to structure their sessions along these broad lines, otherwise the conversation is likely to lose focus and fail to achieve the desired outcomes. Although these points are very broad they emphasise a disciplined approach as well as reflection, which is touched on below in our discussion of learning theory and was set out in more detail in Chapter 2.

Coaching through process

Many excellent coaches achieve their results purely by using their coaching skills and have no knowledge whatsoever of the subject matter with which the learner is concerned. In such circumstances, the coach needs questioning and listening skills to challenge beliefs, opinions or attitudes or to be a sounding board. Here the coach is a process person with first-rate process, interpersonal and relationship-building skills and does not need to be a subject expert.

Coaching through content

Many learners also need, or prefer, someone who has relevant experience and a thorough understanding of the subject matter. In this case, the coach needs to coach from process and content. This involves questioning, inspired analysis, guidance, the ability to uncover options and explore different solutions, to guide detailed action planning and follow through back into the work environment.

The following are some different views of the skills required to be a coach:

'The ability to challenge when someone says everything is all right. The skill to probe to see if they are hiding something, or are not aware of things you need to expose. The ability not to anticipate, because you may put something in the mind of the learner that was not there. Sensitivity and discretion are also vital. The coach needs a wide knowledge of the sector to be able to see the learner's behaviour in context. It is essential to have the knowledge and understanding to say here it happens like that and elsewhere like this.' *Jodi Myers, Director of Performing Arts, Royal Festival Hall / South Bank Centre*

'A coach must be able to challenge and get people to look at things in a new way as a critical skill. The most exciting thing is for the learner to go away galvanised with new thoughts on big problems. Typically, in a session I will tackle the learner: 'What are your current bug-bears that you cannot find a way around? Let's unpack it and look at new ways.' Sometimes, I am getting them to recognise things that they did not want to face but that they need to deal with. How do you sort out the finances to manage your budget? How did you deal with the elected member?

'I ask them questions to help them identify the options and get them to think the issue through. I get them to really understand the situation. Often the learner has an expectation that I will develop with them areas they haven't experienced. They want a better self-knowledge or understanding of something. Sometimes, the learner asks what I might do in the situation. I may respond with my personal approach but always put other options to them with equal weight and suggest how other people tackle the same thing. I strenuously avoid the "my way is best" syndrome.' *Debbie Kingsley, a performance coach-mentor to people in arts administration*

'You need a broad interest in problem-solving. You have to be confident enough in yourself to be modest. You also need to be able to communicate at all levels and you need to be analytically capable. People grow in confidence when they are made to feel they can do it. This is primarily what the coaching role is all about. You also need to be critical in a non-judgemental way and drive people to succeed.' *Simone Emmett, an executive coach*

Emmett also says: 'In executive agenda coaching you are often aiming to get a total change in behaviour, you need an attitude shift. This is a behaviour shift over the long term. To do this you need intellectual buy-in, but this brings a short-term change. If you get emotional buy-in, then you get the long-term attitude change.'

COACHING STYLES

Coaching styles span a range from directive to non-directive. When to use a particular style depends on the level of experience and the motivation of the learner and sometimes the circumstances. They apply equally to formal, structured coaching and spontaneous coaching. (I also discussed these styles in Chapter 2.)

Directive styles

If the learner is inexperienced and therefore lacks the necessary skill or knowledge, the coach may need to be more directive. For example, an inexperienced call centre operator may feel that the call did not go well but may not be able to articulate why or what they did wrong. The coaching conversation may go like this:

Coach: Let's analyse your call from XYZ requesting a medical insurance claim form.

Learner: The caller was abrupt and angry – totally unreasonable, in fact.

The learner is unaware of anything they may not have handled well in this call. A tone of voice and body language may project to the coach that they are not ready to accept they could have done something different. Alternatively, they may indicate awareness that they could, indeed, have handled the call differently. In the latter case, the coach can move to a non-directive style.

If it is the former case, the coach needs to build up the learner's awareness through analysis. The coach may also need to come in pretty quickly with a statement of the problem. The coaching conversation may proceed along these lines:

Coach: Let's play the call over ... You are asking some very personal questions. How do you think the caller may feel about this?

Learner: Well, maybe the caller is unhappy about their problem but I am helping them by making the claims process easier.

Coach: Yes, the caller may be in an unhappy state of mind. You also do not know where the caller is ringing from. Maybe they are calling from an open office?

Learner: Oh, I could have explained that if I had some personal information this would make the claims process easier and I could ask them if they were able to speak privately.

The technique illustrated here has the coach using a mixture of statement and questioning to raise the learner's awareness and to get the learner to think through the solution. Nonetheless, the coach is still in directive mode and is aiming to get the learner to recognise the problem and work through the solution so that it suits them and their way of doing things.

Non-directive (role-model) style

When dealing with an experienced high performer, it is more appropriate to adopt a non-directive style and rely mainly on questioning and feedback skills. The more rapidly a coach can move from a directive to a non-directive style, the faster improvement in performance will be achieved. This is because a solution that the learner has worked out for themselves, even if with some guidance, is bound to enjoy greater commitment.

A non-directive style will use questioning to challenge beliefs, or opinions or attitudes, or to be a sounding board. In this situation the learner has total control and responsibility over the learning.

What is the issue? How do you feel about it? What works? What doesn't work? What is the outcome you want? What is stopping you? What are the options? How can you do that? Who can help you? What other resources or support do you need? What effect might that have? What will you do if...? How does that fit with your view of... or your desire to ...? What action will you take? By when? How will you know you have been successful?

Interim styles

There are interim styles that lie between directive and non-directive. These styles will incorporate non-directive-type questions, as above, but will involve the coach in injecting into the session inspired analysis and guidance. The coach may offer different options, give the learner feedback and guide the learner through detailed action planning and follow through back in the work environment.

Coach: How do you feel the meeting went?

Learner: Not well. At first, I thought things were going my way. I was reading the body language. They seemed on my side. Then it all collapsed.

Coach: What was the turning point?

Learner: It was when I introduced the exclusion clause. I think I used the wrong approach.

Coach: What should you have done?

Learner: I have no idea.

Coach: Here are two approaches, you could try. Let's talk them through and see how you could use them . . .

Effective coaches are able to move in and out of each of these styles as circumstances and the learners' needs demand.

WHAT ARE THE SKILLS AND COMPETENCIES REQUIRED TO BE A SUCCESSFUL COACH?

In all of these styles, coaches need to deploy a range of behavioural competencies, as well as knowledge-based ones. The most important are itemised below.

Behavioural competencies

Active listening

Active listening encompasses skills that are usually described as: building rapport, empathising, questioning, suspending judgement and summarising.

Effective active listening is where you:

- listen to hear specific needs
- don't automatically assume that this question or this situation is like any other you have encountered
- give the learner your full attention and take in information that will lead to insightful, personalised responses to their questions
- listen for what the individual is not saying verbally, watching facial expression, body language, and movements, tone of voice and any expressions of emotion
- ask open-ended questions to draw out the learner
- be truly responsive and sensitive to the learner's evolving understanding
- understand that the learner can only respond from their existing knowledge and understanding, and identify where the learner may need some input to be able to give the desired output
- seek the other person's view and bring out for discussion what they may have been thinking but were not articulating
- avoid excessive use of questions, which may discourage the learner from pursuing their own train of thought
- encourage the learner to ask questions, as this helps them clarify their understanding.

THE VIEW FROM THE COACH

In his book *Learning Alliances*, David Clutterbuck offers a helpful way of looking at questioning as 'involving a constant interaction between questioning and understanding. The ultimate test of quality for the coach's questioning is the quality of the resulting questions raised by the learner.'[2]

Building and maintaining trust

Another test for quality can be summed up by Clutterbuck's view that 'constructive challenge is one of the most powerful gifts a coach can give to a learner'. To be able to constructively challenge, you need to first become a critical friend. This involves 'gaining the learner's confidence and trust, both in his or her intentions and in the quality of feedback'.

Giving feedback

Giving and receiving feedback on performance involves:

- praising people and building their confidence
- identifying/helping them identify what they have done well
- being candid with people
- identifying/helping them identify what they need to do differently
- showing someone you are genuinely and personally concerned with their progress
- encouraging someone to give you feedback.

Giving feedback in 'real time' is a highly effective way of helping people learn. For managers, giving feedback in real time is more effective than any performance appraisal once or twice a year can possibly be. It is also tremendously motivating. It creates trust and empathy and helps develop relationships. It creates an optimum problem-solving environment.

Personal development planning

Commonly, when confronted with drawing up a personal development plan, whether this is for coaching or for other purposes, individuals either set out a series of tasks or they identify broad, long-term goals that are admirable in their way but will not help them to learn in the short term.

A partner at PwC describes her first meeting with her coach (some time before she became a partner):

The coach asked me: What drives you?

I said: I want to be a partner.

The coach said: No. What drives you? What I mean is, what can we do together to make your day-to-day work more meaningful?

The partner found this interaction enlightening and immensely helpful. It was for her the starting point to building and implementing a development plan that led her to her ultimate goal.

The reason people find the concept of setting goals difficult is sometimes because they tend to a more intuitive style and they just 'know' what they want to do, or maybe it is because they prefer a fuzzy and unstructured approach. Sometimes, however, it is because they are approaching the planning from a limited perspective.

This is very much the case with delegates on the Public Service Leaders Scheme described in Chapter 7. We saw there that delegates delay setting goals for their personal development plans until they have had exposure to different areas and disciplines. In this way, they set goals from a broader horizon and are able to consider opportunities that they did not previously consider or even know about. It usually takes them six months to craft their plans, and they receive one-to-one coaching support to help them.

In summary, the coach needs to be sensitive to the learner's needs and circumstances when it comes to goal-setting. The coach may also need to enable the learner to develop a broader perspective and must also be able to stimulate the learner's thinking so that they identify meaningful goals.

Other competencies

In Chapter 9, we identified the criteria HR practitioners can use for appointing a coach. For the sake of completeness, I repeat these here so that readers may be able to consider them in the light of the competencies needed to be a coach.

These competencies are:

- *Training and qualifications:* a coach should have relevant training and/or qualifications. This will include being able to administer a range of psychometric and other instruments, and give feedback on these and on 360-degree feedback. The coach should place a high priority on their own continuing professional development.

- *Experience:* the coach may need to have particular functional expertise and industry experience. This will depend on the needs of the learner.

- *Measuring success:* the coach needs to know how to measure the success of a coaching programme and know how to measure their own success. Ideally, the coach themselves should receive coaching, or some form of supervision.

WHAT OF TELEPHONE COACHING?

Telephone coaching is used extensively, and the time and cost advantages it offers make it certain that its use will continue to grow. There is an obvious point of difference between telephone and face-to-face coaching: the loss of appearance, facial expression and gesticulations. Does this point of difference demand different skill sets from those referred to above?

Writing in *Now Hear This*, Jeannie Davis[3] believes: 'You communicate at about 40% of your ability when on the telephone because your facial expressions and gesticulations cannot be seen.' In her research, she has identified that most people place appearance and attitude as the most important characteristics of face-to-face communication, especially for creating a good first impression. It might seem logical to assume from this that communication suffers without the visual input. However, anecdotal evidence and other research, including that from Davies herself, indicates that our senses undergo a major shift and we find other ways of discerning the messages that are communicated visually.

Mike Travis, a US-based executive coach who coaches extensively by telephone, offers this view:

> *Working by telephone, I've become a much more acute non-verbal listener. What do I mean? Well, I would equate it with the extra sense(s) that a blind person develops. Could you imagine feeling more 'exposed' talking to a blind person than to someone who can see you? Body language can be revealing, but it can also be blocking and protective or even help to keep up a front. I believe one can gain extraordinary listening skills coaching by telephone (inflection, pace, etc) to truly pick up 'non-verbal' (the way the words are spoken) by practice. I can hear doubt, confidence, excitement, energy and much more.*

The power of language becomes particularly important in the absence of visual communication. Using the same kind of words and expressions as the learner is important. Using vivid, descriptive language helps put ideas across. Using words that are unambiguous is also important.

Care needs to be taken over rate of speech. It is estimated that the brain can assimilate speech at a much faster rate than we can produce the words. When you consider this, together with the fact that about 25 per cent of audibility is lost over the telephone, it is clear that particular attention needs to be paid to finding the right pace. Too slow, and you may irritate or even lose the listener. Too fast, and you may not be understood. Mirroring someone's pace and also their tone and inflection, always useful techniques for building rapport, are especially effective in telephone interactions.

Another interesting aspect to consider is whether the loss of visual input affects how forthcoming people are prepared to be. This varies according to the person and the circumstances. Some people find it is easier to tell or hear 'the truth' on the telephone and to say things that they might feel embarrassed about in a face-to-face situation. Others find it is easier to deceive.

Tony Jackson, a UK-based executive coach who coaches extensively by telephone, believes you need to have especially acute communication skills when coaching by telephone to ensure you are sensitive to how people are reacting and know how to deal with it.

From my own experience of telephone coaching, I find that it is even more important to give positive, verbal strokes than in face-to-face situations. When you can see someone, their body language can let you know if they have warmed to you, if they think you are stimulating them, and so on. If you are speaking to someone who has good control over their tone of voice, you can come away from what might have otherwise seemed like a successful telephone meeting wondering if they thought you were a complete idiot. Finding the right way of giving some praise and positive feedback that is sincere and not condescending is vital on the telephone to build a long-term relationship.

Do you need to know what someone looks like?

When you meet someone face to face, your appearance determines the impression you make. What happens without this visual input? Views seem to differ quite widely, leading me to the conclusion that it is a matter of personal preference. Some suggest that many people come across on the telephone as being more confident because they don't have to worry about their appearance. In such cases, the telephone is less of a threat, and this encourages people to experiment more. Many coaches find that removing the visual input encourages them to listen and concentrate more intensely. Writing in *Training Journal*, Chris Carling[4] examined this issue by asking his clients for their views. He reports one person who preferred not to know what he looked like, another who had printed his photograph out from his website and another who insisted on meeting him first before commencing the coaching.

What are the skills required to coach people in different countries?

One of the advantages of telephone coaching is that it can so easily cross boundaries. In these circumstances, the coach requires a good understanding of cultural differences and a keen awareness of the nuance of language. When coaching those for whom English may not be their usual business language, the coach needs to pay particular attention to how they express themselves, taking care to adapt their vocabulary and range of expression and avoiding the use of jargon and colloquial expressions.

Coaches who work across national borders need to be attuned to the culture of that country and to their way of doing business.

In summary, telephone coaches require the same skill sets and competencies as when coaching face to face. It is the emphasis that is different, with telephone coaches needing to present as complete a picture of themselves as possible through their voice and how they handle the call, so as to compensate for the loss of visual input. A cross-cultural understanding may also be necessary for those who coach people in different countries.

Even where webcams, or indeed video-conferencing is used, this does not adequately enable people to read one another's visual body language. I believe, therefore, that many of the points discussed here apply also to coaching online. Coaching online is discussed fully in Chapter 8, where I also set out some additional competencies required of the coach.

KNOWLEDGE-BASED COMPETENCIES

As well as being masters of certain skills and having the right level of training, functional expertise and possible business experience, coaches need a theoretical knowledge and practical understanding of two important areas: how people learn, and what motivates them to learn. These competencies are equally as valuable to the HR professional.

Learning

It is a truism that coaching is about learning. Many readers will already be aware of learning theories and, for those who are less familiar with them, I cannot possibly portray them adequately in the space available here. However, I feel my analysis of coaching would be incomplete without, at least, some mention of them. I therefore identify the key points and summarise the practical applications they have spawned. I am greatly helped here by the research, 'How do People Learn?' commissioned by the CIPD and conducted by the University of Cambridge.[5]

Much learning theory is based on an explanation of knowledge given by the Oxford philosopher Gilbert Ryle in 1949,[6] according to which there is a difference between 'knowing how' and 'knowing that'. This distinction is valuable because it helps us to understand what makes learning effective. Knowing how is inextricably linked to performance – to competent practice – and therefore cannot be separated from the context in which it arises or is applied. It is the tacit knowledge produced by solving problems of a practical rather than abstract nature and extends beyond common sense into the mastery of situations.

This distinction enables us to see immediately how the primary focus of coaching needs to enable someone to 'know how'.

There are over 50 recognised and reputable theories of learning. The 'How do People Learn' report has structured this whole body of theory into four 'clusters', as follows:

Learning as behaviour

Proponents of this group of theories believe we learn by doing. Case studies and action learning are two of the practical applications that come from this cluster of theories.

Learning by understanding

This is often referred to as cognitive learning. It is about learning the content. The university or classroom lecture is based on this model.

Learning as knowledge construction

This is basically the theory of learning by making mistakes, and role-playing and simulations are some key practical applications. Theorists here build on the learning by understanding theories but say that to be effective you have to be able to adapt the learning to your own particular way of doing things. They say that you have to be able to try things out and make mistakes in order to assimilate the learning as part of your normal behaviour. However, if you make the same mistake twice, this implies you have not learned.

David A. Kolb developed a model known as the experiential learning cycle, which depicts how experience is transformed, via reflection, into concepts that guide future activity and hence new experiences. It shows that learning is a process, not a one-off activity. The Kolb learning cycle is a valuable tool for helping people learn, as is the reflective learning cycle set out in Chapter 2.

Learning as a social experience

Social theories do not contradict the other theories but add to them. Followers of the social model of learning argue that learning is inherently a social experience. We learn through and with others, and what we choose to learn depends on the communities we choose to join. This cluster of learning theories is satisfied by courses, conferences, online chat rooms, online and offline discussion networks, and so on.

These four clusters of learning enable us to understand that different situations demand different approaches to encouraging and supporting learning. This depends not just on the learner but on what is to be taught and the situation in which it is taught. Driving instruction, for example, is behaviourist: you don't need or want to construct knowledge about cars and motoring – you just need to know how and when to change gear without thinking about it.

Learning styles

One of the most important practical applications to derive from learning theory is that learners have characteristic strengths and preferences in the ways they take in and process information, known as learning styles. Just as an understanding of the learning clusters discussed above enables us to design learning to suit different situations, so learning styles are about designing learning to suit the individual learner.

Learners are not necessarily fixed in one style and will benefit from exposure to a full range of approaches. This approach to learning emphasises the fact that individuals perceive and process information in very different ways. The learning styles theory implies that how much individuals learn has more to do with whether the learning experience is geared toward their particular style of learning than whether or not they are 'smart'.

The concept of learning styles is rooted in the classification of psychological types. It is based on research demonstrating that, as a result of heredity, upbringing and current environmental demands, different individuals have a tendency to perceive and process information differently. There are a number of theorists, academics and consultants who have developed learning styles models. They tend to classify learning styles in one of two ways:

1 Perceiving and processing information

There are two categories of perceivers: concrete and abstract. Concrete perceivers absorb information through direct experience, by doing, acting, sensing and feeling. Abstract perceivers, however, take in information through analysis, observation and thinking.

There are also two categories of processor: active and reflective. Active processors make sense of an experience by immediately using the new information. Reflective processors make sense of an experience by reflecting on and thinking about it.

2 Using different channels of perception

The second way of classifying learning styles is by reflecting different channels of perception (seeing, hearing, touch, moving), as in the accompanying table.

Learning style	Preference for information acquisition
Visual/Verbal	Prefers to read information
Visual/Non-verbal	Uses graphics or diagrams to represent information
Auditory/Verbal	Prefers to listen to information
Tactile/Kinaesthetic	Prefers physical hands-on experience

Most people find it helpful to identify their learning preferences. That is not to say that people cannot learn from situations that do not suit their preferences, but experience has shown that people learn more effectively if they can choose learning opportunities that suit their preferred learning styles.

Identifying and understanding their own learning preferences helps learners identify the methods they are more comfortable with and understand why they find it easier to learn from certain methods and certain activities than others.

Alerting learners to their present learning style preferences, through learning-style diagnostics, also encourages them to broaden their repertoire of learning skills so that they can better accommodate a wider mix of learning methods.

It bears repetition that knowing how to learn is one of the most important skills needed in business today. It should be an essential first stage in any coaching assignment, where the learner has not previously been through such an exercise. This will help the learner get the most from the coaching; it will help the coach adapt to the learner's styles and preferences; and it will also enable the learner to appreciate how to keep on learning throughout their lives.

Coaches and HR practitioners can benefit from understanding their own learning styles, so that we do not fall into the trap of designing learning around methods that suit our own preferences.

A very important point I would like to make regarding learning styles is that as we progress in our working lives, our learning preferences become more defined, and we have greater need of being able to choose those that suit us best.

Motivation

The motivation to learn is important, and it is essential for the coach to key into what motivates the learner and to understand their current level of motivation. Research evidence suggests that learners are primarily motivated by interest, enjoyment, satisfaction, recognition and challenge, as well as having clear goals and being able to see results. These 'intrinsic' motivators are generally found to be more important than financial rewards.

The coach needs to recognise these feelings and create coaching that satisfies these motivational needs.

Diagnostic instruments are often helpful in identifying someone's value systems and motivations.

The coach needs also to be aware that it is part of their role to make sure the coaching boosts the learner's self-esteem and self-confidence and raises their level of awareness.

The ARCS Model for Motivation (Attention, Relevance, Confidence, Satisfaction) developed by John Keller,[7] sets out a list of characteristics to which attention should be paid when designing or writing effective learning programs. The model is based on existing research on psychological motivation. Keller's terms can be described as follows:

- *Attention:* gaining and keeping the learner's attention.
- *Relevance:* attention and motivation will not be maintained unless the learner believes the training is relevant.
- *Confidence:* learners must feel capable of achieving the objectives within a reasonable timeframe and by expending a reasonable level of effort. In technology-based training programs, students should be given estimates of the time required to complete lessons or a measure of their progress through the program.
- *Satisfaction:* learners must obtain some type of satisfaction or reward from the

learning experience. This can be in the form of entertainment, such as an animation offering congratulations or a sense of achievement such as a test result or certificate or in the form of praise from a line manager. The best way for learners to achieve satisfaction is for them to find their new skills immediately useful and advantageous to their work.

KEY LEARNING POINTS

The new coaching model emphasises the developmental benefits of coaching. It stresses the importance of following a process and of being non-directive.

A coach can coach from process alone and know nothing of the subject-matter with which the learner is concerned.

Much coaching, however, is also concerned with content and the coach may need to be a subject expert, or be on the same level or have a certain background in order to understand the learner, relate to them and challenge them effectively.

The coach needs to be able to switch between non-directive, directive and interim coaching styles to suit the learner, and should use directive styles only when all else fails.

It is possible to identify a range of core competencies that are required to be an effective coach. These include behavioural competencies such as active listening, being a critical friend, giving feedback and setting goals. Other competencies include training, qualifications, functional expertise, industry experience, measuring success. Areas of knowledge include how people learn and what motivates people.

Telephone coaching requires broadly the same skill sets. Telephone coaches need to be able to compensate for the loss of appearance, gestures and facial expressions in the way they present themselves. This requires exceptionally acute listening skills. They also need to be able to engage the learner through the way they use their voice and through the use of language. Those who coach across national boundaries need to have cross-cultural sensitivity and understanding. Many of the differences between telephone and face-to-face coaching apply to online coaching.

NOTES AND REFERENCES

1 ZEUS P. *and* SKIFFINGTON S. (1999) 'The new coaching model' *HR Monthly.* November 1999.

2 CLUTTERBUCK D. (1998) *Learning Alliances.* London, CIPD.

3 DAVIS J. (2002) *Beyond 'Hello'.* Colorado, Now Hear This Inc, Aurora.

4 CARLING C. (2001) 'Reflections of a phone coach: does coaching by phone really work? *Training Journal.*

5 REYNOLDS J., CALEY L. and MASON R. (2002) *How People Learn.* London, CIPD. A research report prepared by the Chartered Institute of Personnel and Development for Cambridge Programme for Industry.

6   RYLE G. (1949) *The Concept of Mind.* Harmondsworth, Penguin.

7   KELLER J. (1979) *Keller's ARCS Model of Motivation.* Florida, Florida State University.
    www.ittheory.com/keller1.htm

11

Viewing the coach

We turn now to looking at coaching from the learner's perspective in order to help HR practitioners work effectively with learners in determining when coaching is appropriate for them and how to get the most from it.

At the very outset the learner considering the coaching option needs to have the following questions answered:

Will coaching help me? How do I know if I am ready for coaching? How do I choose a coach? How can I ensure I get the best from coaching? What is it like to experience effective coaching? How will I know the coaching has been successful? When does coaching go wrong, and how can I guard against this?

Many of these questions have been addressed elsewhere in this book and those answers do not need repeating. My aim in this chapter is therefore to add to what has already been examined and to set out viewpoints and guidance on what it is like to experience coaching in order to inform the decisions of whether coaching is the right solution and how to choose the right coach.

WILL COACHING BENEFIT ME?

The potential benefits of coaching have been discussed in Chapter 3. Nonetheless, let us reconsider them briefly here. After all, success demands buy-in, which requires the learner to be convinced of the benefits of coaching at the outset. The research conducted into the effectiveness of coaching shows that among the benefits to executives were improvements in: working relationships with direct reports (reported by 77 per cent of executives), working relationships with immediate supervisors (71 per cent), teamwork (67 per cent), working relationships with peers (63 per cent), job satisfaction (61 per cent), conflict reduction (52 per cent), organisational commitment (44 per cent), working relationships with clients (37 per cent), and so on.

As discussed already, in an ideal learning organisation that is receptive to and gets the most out of coaching there will be a strategy in place that aligns coaching with its organisational goals. This will help to determine learning needs for both the organisation and the individual, and when coaching is appropriate to meet them.

For example, the managers within an organisation seek a goal of improving sales performance as part of their strategy to increase market share from 12 to 20 per cent over three years. They agree a learning strategy that includes training supported by coaching for their three sales managers and fifteen regional sales executives. This learning strategy includes a detailed statement of the skill sets the staff are expected to acquire or enhance and the targets they are to aim for. Once corporate goals and individual needs have been identified, it is then necessary to determine whether coaching is the optimum learning solution for that person, in those particular set of circumstances, to meet the goals.

HOW CAN THE LEARNER GET THE MOST FROM COACHING?

Having decided that coaching does provide some or all of the solution, it is then necessary to try to establish it and manage it in a way that will ensure success.

The scenarios presented here convey something of the experience of both effective and ineffective coaching. These insights should inform our understanding of what coaching entails and help both to identify when coaching is an inappropriate solution and also to guard against choosing the wrong coach or the wrong coaching method.

What is it like to experience effective coaching?

One executive describes how she felt about being coached:

Being coached is a wonderfully egotistical experience. Complete attention is devoted to you. It is about you and for you. In this new model of coaching, in contrast to remedial coaching, it is positive evidence that the organisation is investing in you and is concerned about your development.

Annie Devoy, PWC Director in Tax and Legal Services, talking at a Aurora (previously Busygirl) meeting in May 2002 , said of the external coaching she had received: 'The coach has had an input that I did not realise she would have. I definitely enjoy my job more now'

A senior manager from an American fast-moving consumer goods conglomerate believes that some coaching he received:

helped me see things more clearly. You are so close to your behaviour you cannot discern it. It is good to have someone challenge you and ask questions and make you think differently about your behaviour and the responses you get from people. It is particularly effective when you are asked really good, fundamental questions. These do not have to be specifically about content. The coaching made me be more flexible and get more enjoyment from my work.

Another senior executive from an American high-tech company feels that coaching is especially beneficial when the coach asks provocative questions to make you think more broadly:

It is how you do what you do. Lots of people have the same 'whats and whys'. It is particularly important to keep your mind open for other people's perspectives. So much is built on points of view, and people take entrenched views and stop listening. They stop listening to new ideas. You need to hold ideas more loosely and listen to and get better solutions. This is what I got out of the coaching.

One senior manager wrote the following in his evaluation report of the coaching he had received:

We spent some time throughout the coaching looking at how I present my views, so that I achieve an objective rather than winning an argument. This is still hard for me to do because it is in my nature to analyse and respond to the facts as I see them. However, I can see more clearly that it is not necessarily the way others will respond, and that dwelling on the problems can get in the way of others accepting the proposed solutions. Writing about the achievements of the executive committee and each of the research and development teams showed me that there are positive achievements to talk about, and I need to emphasise this in future.

One manager described how a coach helped him by coaching from the angle of a psychotherapist. The coaching was geared to business results, but the learner was at a difficult stage in his personal life and had issues around relationships and life direction. The coach enabled him to think through the personal issues, handle these better and make some decisions. As a result, he was able to deal with work better and achieve his business goals.

What is it like to experience poor coaching?

Coaching does not always work out so well, however. In one scenario, three new personnel managers were recruited into a very large and long-established organisation. The personnel director was keen to change the style of the personnel department, and recruited these new managers with that remit. All three were experienced and professionally qualified. They were paid considerably more than the existing staff, who were not professionally qualified and who had a more old-fashioned view of the role of the personnel manager. The existing staff were aggressive towards and unwelcoming of the new recruits, so coaching was arranged for the new recruits to help them deal with the situation. The new recruits were keen to receive this coaching, believing it would help them deal better with what they described as an 'emotionally charged working environment'.

One of the recruits valued the coaching in many ways and felt it achieved many benefits for the department, but she resented the personal path the coach had insisted on leading her down. The coach's approach was that she should express her feelings about the working environment and talk about her personal emotions and feelings. This person felt such an approach to be intrusive and completely misjudged for her personally. She had welcomed the idea of a coach to help her through the situation but did not welcome the approach she was offered. She would have preferred a methodology that helped her think through the strategies she should have been adopting at work.

Another example concerns a senior banking executive whose organisation set up executive coaching for all staff at a senior level. The executive was receptive to the idea until his first session with the coach. It was a lengthy getting-to-know-one-another session, and the coach was delving into all aspects of the executive's life. This perfectly confident, happily married and well-balanced person, who felt sure he was organising all aspects of his life pretty well, felt immediately resentful at being asked about his finances and other personal matters. He became especially alarmed when the coach reassured him, in a conspiratorial manner, that he should feel completely at ease about discussing all aspects of his life, and asked him if he was having an affair. The coach apparently advised him to feel free to tell all, presumably secure in the sanctity of the confessional!

My analysis of these situations is that, in both cases, the coaches had a set path and a predetermined methodology that they followed rigidly. They both misread their learners and failed to take the time up-front to build the relationship, determine the coaching methodology that would suit the learner and put in place a learner-driven coaching plan.

Another situation concerns a learner who was writing a book and engaged a coach to support him in this endeavour. It turned out, however, that the coach lacked fundamental coaching skills, with the result that she demoralised rather than helped the learner. For example, whenever the learner wished to discuss an idea the coach responded in a directive and dogmatic manner, such as 'Oh, that's a bad idea – you should do this or that.'

A common problem that arises in coaching or usually, specifically, mentoring relationships where the learners are young, inexperienced people is that they do not know how to use the time properly. One senior executive in the performing arts often finds that the learners he mentors do not use the sessions productively enough. They do not ask the right questions or discuss the right topics. Undoubtedly, this problem arises because the learner is too inexperienced to know what to discuss. An effective coach should be more skilful at finding out what the learner needs to know.

What other circumstances cause coaching to fail?

Almost all coaches have come across situations where the learner is unreceptive to coaching. This may result from the manner in which the coaching has been set up by the organisation or from organisational issues, or it may arise from the learner's perception of coaching: thinking of it, perhaps, as a stigma.

One coach described a situation where she was engaged to help a learner implement his personal development plan. He had drafted this together with his line manager and the HR manager following a 360-degree feedback exercise. The plan identified some interpersonal and behavioural competencies that he needed to adopt, especially when dealing with his staff. The overall organisational goal was to move managers away from command-and-control to collaborative leadership styles. The coach realised from the outset that the learner was merely going along with the coaching, probably because he felt he had to, but had no real desire to adopt these new behaviours and did not understand the need for them. He participated in the coaching sessions in a reluctant manner, did not work on the action plans, and his staff were unable to discern any improvement in management style.

It is easy to speculate on what the coach might have done differently, but undoubtedly the underlying problem was how the coaching had been arranged by the organisation.

Is the learner ready for coaching?

The learner has to be ready for coaching and ready to make it work. Those who are 'ready' will meet the following criteria. They will:

- believe learning and self-development are a priority
- identify business results that they want to achieve as a result of having coaching or have some particular needs that they wish to address through coaching

- be willing to change their behaviour at work, try different ways of doing things and examine new perspectives
- regard the coaching as a partnership and be prepared to put time, thought and effort into the relationship
- commit to the coaching and undertake to keep the coaching appointments, do any preparation needed for each session and follow through on agreed action plans
- be prepared for the coach to challenge them
- discuss their relationship with the coach, giving the coach feedback on what they like or don't like about their approach, and letting them know if they are unwilling to try ideas and seek alternatives
- be open with the coach and admit concerns and fears, on the understanding that the coach will keep the conversations completely confidential.

Working through these criteria with someone can be a useful way of finding out if they are ready for coaching. Perhaps more importantly, it can also serve to raise their awareness of the effort and preparation they themselves will need to put into coaching. Coaching will not be the right solution for the executive if, after the HR manager has discussed learning solutions with them (using a coaching style) and has spread the coaching message throughout the organisation, they do not agree with the above and demonstrate any of the following:

- the conviction that coaching does not work
- the belief that a successful person who tries to change the way they behave part-way through their career is likely to damage their own effectiveness
- the concern that they are really busy and don't know how they can fit in coaching sessions without sacrificing some of what little free time they have
- agreement that, of course, coaching can be really helpful but nonetheless the view that no one can really understand what they do and the way they operate, and that it isn't appropriate to have a stranger at their elbow
- the belief that coaching is helpful for most people but not necessary for them as they are already a high performer.

Obtaining the learner's views on the above can be a useful way of finding out whether someone is ready for coaching. Perhaps more importantly, it can also serve to raise someone's awareness of the effort and preparation they themselves will need to put into coaching.

HOW TO CHOOSE A COACH

Once it has been determined that coaching is the right solution, the learner then needs to choose the coach. This should be a carefully thought-out exercise, since mistakes are expensive in terms both of wasted cash and lost opportunity.

Before meeting prospective coaches, the learner, together with their HR manager, should be clear about the following:

- What methodology will suit the learner?
- What coaching roles (see Witherspoon's continuum of coaching roles in Chapter 3) best suit the learner's needs?
- Does the learner want help in identifying his or her most pressing business challenges and in exploring alternative strategies for tackling them?
- Does the learner want to consider a wide range of business and personal issues, such as achieving a more satisfying balance between accomplishing increased business results and leading a more fulfilled personal life?
- Is the learner only concerned with accomplishing specific results, or is he or she open to broader life changes?
- Does the learner need or want someone who has particular functional expertise or business experience?
- Does the learner want someone who can be a confidential sounding board who will help in seeing different perspectives in how they approach issues?

The learner should be presented with a shortlist of three coaches to meet. The following ideas may help the learner to decide which coach is likely to suit them best:

- Do you warm to the coach?
- Do they seem to be listening to you?
- Do you feel 'safe' with them – for example, do they come across as non-judgemental, Do they empathise with you, do they appear supportive?
- Do they ask you lots of questions and are these questions challenging and perceptive?
- Do they seem to understand you and your needs?
- Why do they coach: is to help others or themselves?

Ask them:

- How many executives have they coached, and for how long?
- What level were they, and what kind of positions did they hold?
- What boundaries do they draw around the coaching they provide, and how do they ensure they keep to these?
- What are their qualifications for coaching?
- What other training have they had?
- How do they maintain their professional development?
- What business experience have they had? Ask for more details about this and especially for their experience of managing people, or other resources, if this is relevant.
- What is the coach's specialty?

- What three issues do they see most frequently across all the executives they coach?
- What specific goals do they help learners with most often?
- How do they decide on a coaching strategy for the executive?
- When do they turn down a prospective learner?
- How do they determine whether someone is not ready for coaching?
- How do they structure a session? If the coach is experienced, ask them to describe three successful coaching assignments.
- How do they monitor whether the coaching is achieving its goals?
- How do they measure their own success?
- What do they do if they feel the relationship isn't working?

Conclusion

Coaching can be an enormously powerful tool, but its success demands understanding and commitment from the learner. Although they don't need to be technical experts, anyone intending to use coaching should be familiar with the subject matter of this chapter even if they don't read the entire book. The process outlined above takes the learner through the benefits of coaching; the discipline of ensuring that organisational and personal goals are best met through coaching; some understanding of the process to appreciate what makes coaching work or fail; and the learner attitudes that impede progress. The final section illustrates, through some questions to be posed to the coach and to the learner/HR department, the disciplined approach to choosing an effective coach.

KEY LEARNING POINTS

The learner must be convinced that coaching will help them at the outset.

Academic research supports the view that coaching can be an extremely effective learning tool.

Implement coaching if it provides the optimal solution to meet clearly stated individual and organisational needs.

It helps a new learner to have some idea of what coaching is like, eg meeting those who have passed through coaching or reading of their experiences can prepare the ground.

Good coaching experiences are characterised by good rapport, with the coach stimulating the learner and sensitively challenging ideas and beliefs.

Poor coaching experiences are characterised by poor rapport, insensitivity and inflexibility.

The learner must be receptive to coaching for it to be successful; they must believe it can work and be prepared to commit effort to make it do so.

Choosing the right coach demands more than just a chat and making a decision based on who is most affable. The learner and HR professional must prepare appropriate questions in the light of learning goals and needs.

NOTES AND REFERENCES

1   See www.manchesterusa.com

12

The HR coach

Technology and the changing business environment have provided the HR function with the opportunity to shed much of its bureaucratic and administrative burden and take on an increased strategic, advisory role in the organisation. The role of HR began in recruitment, payroll, and establishing and managing terms and conditions, and then in disciplining and firing staff. It developed into more strategic areas such as motivation, training and manpower planning, but much of the energy of the role has remained focused on the basic administrative burden.

Nowadays a substantial part of these roles, such as recruitment, performance appraisal and pay reviews has been moved back into the hands of line managers, albeit supported by HR personnel. Many HR departments now act as consultants, providing services such as training and development, recruitment and advice on company policy or employment law. Various technological solutions, such as intranets, enable managers and staff to take responsibility for their own administration and have made the procedural elements of HR simpler and less labour-intensive. In the case study on Lloyds TSB, we saw how the HR call centre provides advice both to line managers and employees on a wide range of HR matters.

The changes in the role of HR are not just structural. Especially in those organisations that lean towards more collaborative styles of leadership, HR now assists the organisation in becoming competitive by developing the workforce, business objectives and long-range strategies to support profitability. It has moved much more towards the centre of the stage as a part of formulating policy. Strategic recruitment policies, management succession planning, developing the internal brand and organisational design are now often within the remit of HR. Under the old model, HR professionals used to spend all their time policing the implementation of HR initiatives. Now they work on the strategy formulation, help design the process and empower line managers to get on with it.

We saw in Chapter 4 that the human resource team at BTexact Technologies focuses on enabling and facilitating people policies, as opposed to policing and implementation. To operate in this way requires greater skills of visioning, innovation and influencing.

Mike Laws of Ernst & Young describes the HR function in a similar way, emphasising that the HR role is not policing initiatives but visioning change and then enabling and facilitating it. As he says, 'In this organisation, you stimulate the thinking and work where the energy is. It is definitely not about telling.'

These changes have enabled human resource professionals to become integrated and valued members of the management team. However, this broader role also demands a much broader skill mix, which includes consulting, coaching and communication, along with an appreciation of general business issues.

Paul Turner, Group HR Business Director at Lloyds TSB, was quoted in *People Management*[1] as saying:

> *Those who work in HR nowadays need the imagination of Steven Spielberg, the incisiveness of Jeremy Paxman, the interviewing skills of Oprah Winfrey and the skin of a rhinoceros. While for tiptoeing between the political sensitivities of managers, the grace of Darcey Bussell is hardly any less essential.*

Increasingly, the HR manager is called on to disseminate their knowledge to line management. Thus we have the development of the HR coach who may find themselves in the position of performing informal, 'spontaneous coaching' or who may actually work on a formal basis as an internal coach with line management.

To a certain extent seeing the HR manager as a coach to the line manager is nothing new. HR professionals have always focused on helping managers by directing their attention to the consequences of decisions about people and the way they interact. They have also always provided feedback to managers about the impact of their personal and behavioural style on others. Indeed, using coaching and consulting techniques with line managers was one of the key elements of the Master's Degree in Manpower Studies (human resource management) I undertook nearly 20 years ago. From my own personal experience, I always saw it as a critical part of my role, as an HR manager, to work in partnership with line managers, asking challenging questions and getting them to reflect on how they handled situations. Such a role has always required sensitivity and understanding about how people respond to feedback.

Where things are different now is that HR, having had the burden of administration, implementation and procedure lightened, can focus much more on partnering line managers to develop their people management skills and make them self-sufficient in this respect.

To be an effective internal coach the HR manager needs to be seen as credible, non-judgemental and discreet. Many line managers may feel embarrassed to admit needing help; they may worry about confidentiality; they may worry that a note will end up on their personnel file. The HR manager who takes on a coaching role needs to be able to overcome these fears. This is done through reputation and standing in the organisation, through genuine integrity and by an ever-continuing campaign of persuasion supported by a track record of living up to promises. In the final analysis, any manager will only work effectively with a colleague they trust, and working to establish trust is the start of carrying out an HR role successfully.

The most common coaching scenarios revolve around people-management issues. Especially in modern organisations with fairly flat hierarchies, many people take on management responsibilities at an advanced stage in their careers. They may have had no previous management skills training, and coaching may need to make up for this. In addition to such general skills development, the line manager or supervisor may seek input about handling a particular situation or may need reassurance that their approach is along the right lines.

In response to such situations the role of the HR professional is to provide options and recommend resources; they can offer opinions; they can provide a different perspective, can challenge the line manager and encourage them to confront performance issues; they can answer questions. But, ultimately, the decision should rest with the manager. Coaching rather than telling will be more productive for the line manager as well as for the relationship with them.

One of the most important factors the internal HR manager brings to the coaching role is a knowledge of the organisation and the impact of the manager within that environment and on staff. But to be a good internal coach you must also possess process skills, know about diagnostic instruments and goal-setting strategies, have access to a variety of resources, be knowledgeable about management models and techniques and be clear on the competencies that have an impact on the bottom line.

Both John Bailey at KPMG and Mike Laws at Ernst & Young have internal coaching roles. John Bailey acts as career development coach to a number of partners and also to the other internal career coaches. Mike Laws meets one partner every six weeks and discusses his business relationships with him. Together they work through how the partner can be of help to his client and what the relationship needs to be like. The partner believes he has won extra business as a result of the coaching.

If the HR manager does work as an internal coach to the line manager, it is important to make this explicit and define the boundaries of the relationship. Are you a trusted adviser, critical friend and sounding board or is this a full coaching relationship? Do you listen to and provide feedback yourself or do you help the manager obtain 360-degree feedback and develop action plans to increase their capability as a leader? The relationship can be informal: it does not necessarily need a specific 'contract' covering issues such as where to meet, how often and for how long, or prior agreement on the specific focus and goals of each session. But it works best if it is explicit and defined.

One thing is certain: for a coaching role to succeed, the line manager must take the initiative in seeking the assistance of the HR manager, rather than the latter imposing their services. An aggressive approach reinforces feelings of distrust that are representative of a failed relationship with HR. In addition to the ability to build a relationship of trust with line managers, it is also important for the HR manager to combine both process and coaching skills. Even possessing good process skills or strong strategic skills is not sufficient to achieve success without the addition of sound coaching skills that enable the HR professional to interact effectively with other professionals within the organisation.

In the modern corporation, people are now seen as part of the asset base, but the process of managing people is still seldom viewed as business-critical. *Director Magazine* (October 2002) reported that only 18 per cent of the companies in the UK's FTSE 100 index have an HR director on the board.[2] In the same article, Duncan Brown, the Assistant Director General of the CIPD, is quoted as saying that 'the profession has spent too much time talking about being on the board and too little devising strategies to get there'. One of the central themes of this book is that the skills of coaching have the potential to revolutionise the HR relationship with the managers and executives of their organisation.

In emphasising the importance of HR deploying coaching skills, I do not want to suggest that the HR professional is somehow different from other executives. There is considerable scope for HR people themselves to benefit from an external coach or mentor, taking the lead from how coaching and mentoring have affected the arts industry (Chapter 4). The argument of this book is that a coaching style, a coaching culture and formal coaching have a valuable role to play in all organisational functions.

It is also important to emphasise that the benefits of coaching are not confined to large organisations. As reported in *Director Magazine* (October 2002), the CIPD held a meeting for HR managers in small and medium-sized enterprises (SMEs), which was attended by 400 people. 'They were very keen to discover how they could tap into external support to help them do more,' says Duncan Brown. Most SMEs cannot afford HR directors, yet people issues are actually their primary concern.[3]

HR professionals in SMEs have an advantage over those in larger enterprises: they are closer to the MD and usually have a far more informal structure that facilitates greater input from departmental heads. It is therefore likely that smaller enterprises will actually prove extremely fertile ground for the new ideas on coaching. However, the HR professional in an SME also suffers the disadvantage of not having other personnel professionals to consult. Most personnel people in lone HR roles feel isolated, even lonely, in their role and often fear their professional development is hampered by not having other professionals with whom to exchange ideas.

As a result they can find it intimidating to introduce initiatives at the cutting-edge of thinking in management development and feel a particularly strong need to sponsor initiatives that will provide rapid results to support their position in the organisation. However, the coaching approach is ideal in such circumstances simply because much can be done that is very low risk to the organisation, and the cultural change can be introduced gradually.

Indications are that the HR agenda is changing. I hope that this book will be helpful to HR practitioners and line managers by putting into perspective the opportunities that are now available for optimising the way the people of the business are managed.

NOTES AND REFERENCES

1   RANA E. (2002) 'What can we do to make it a happen?' *People Management*. 16 May.

2   MURPHY C. (2002) 'Careering towards a crisis?' *Director Magazine*. October. p82.

3   MURPHY C. (2002) 'Careering towards a crisis?' *Director Magazine*. October. p82.

13

What does the future look like for coaching?

Coaching can be compared to a technological innovation whose use develops fairly slowly as acceptance and expertise develop, but that grows very rapidly once a threshold is reached. I see coaching as having attained the level where very rapid growth is possible, as there is now a critical mass of expertise and experience that demonstrates that it is effective. I strongly believe, and hope to have persuaded the reader of this also, that the coaching tool can help businesses to be competitive, as well as helping people individually attain their potential. I also believe that coaching suits the attitudes as well as the needs of our times. It fits into our perspectives of our working lives and what we wish to get out of them. It also provides a more appropriate way of managing and developing staff in modern organisations, and it enables the (increasingly important) sharing of knowledge in the organisation.

HOW DOES COACHING SUIT THE ATTITUDES AND NEEDS OF OUR TIMES?

Back in the 1980s and 1990s, HR professionals addressed 'work and family' issues and started looking at how we could go about introducing family-friendly policies. Then, in the mid-1990s, concern about stress in organisations and the effects of the long-hours culture widened the debate to 'work–life balance' issues. As a partial response to this, we now have new employment legislation giving increased rights to leave and time off for various family reasons. However, the work–life balance debate runs into many philosophical and practical difficulties, because people see it as favouring women with children and disadvantaging everyone else. As the debate continues, there is now increasing evidence that many women and men alike would prefer to trade some of their pay for increased flexibility over their working hours, and in some cases a reduction in hours, to suit a variety of needs and circumstances.

So the focus of attention has moved on to 'personal productivity', which is about giving people scope to organise themselves, their time and their lives, and giving them control over what they do at work and how they do it, while at the same time providing the tools and the boundaries that will enable them to reach their potential. Organisations benefit from the productivity gains, while new communication technologies enable people to work more flexibly without damaging the effectiveness of the organisation: just think of the number of people who are able to work from home for part of the time.

To achieve the benefits of enhanced personal productivity, organisations need a leadership model based on collaborative coaching styles. Moreover, 'personal productivity' also offers more choice to people, who therefore benefit from seeking the support of effective coaches and mentors to advance their careers and their lives.

Glenda Stone, CEO and founder of the Aurora women's network,[1] emphasises that this is not about new terms superseding old ones: 'It's about the debate moving on, and one of the key elements in this debate is how career women and men manage a sustainable and rewarding career on their own terms.'

Stone has been keeping a close eye on what is happening in the world of coaching. She sees increasing numbers of coaches entering the market and believes that there is likely to be a major fall-out at some point in the near future. After this she predicts that we will see more speciality coaches and more people forming networks.

My own view is that coaching has now evolved to the point where it has a skill set of its own. This needs to be recognised, and a clear set of quality standards and ethical guidelines should be developed and overseen by a professional body. Such a body would be responsible for training, standards and ethics, and would be a focal point for research, ideas and information. It would enable organisations to identify the successful criteria for organising coaching and avoiding the pitfalls. It would also help guard against malpractice and misrepresentation.

The European Mentoring and Coaching Council, which counts among its trustees and executive board many UK-based luminaries as well as European and international representatives, is well placed to be such a body.

A professional body would also be the natural focus for bringing people together and for debating issues.

A recent teleforum on corporate coaching[2] identified the following issues as being important for debate:

- quantitative and qualitative data related to coaching
- learning around the impact of coaching on corporations
- cross-organisational sharing or ideas and experiences
- thoughts around how we can take forward further research
- connection with others interested in coaching
- discussion around how to track the value of internal/external coaching.

As coaching evolves and increases in popularity, it seems that coaches are developing niches and specialties. This development is likely to accelerate, if, as Stone predicts, people begin to embrace the idea of engaging coaches, personally and outside of work, to help them with different elements of their lives. This is going beyond engaging a 'tennis coach' towards having a coach to help you work through a problem or change in your life, help you deal with a difficult situation, and so on.

From the case studies in this book, we can see that specialty coaching is already a reality. Those that we have mentioned include:

- press relations
- media performance
- heads of small businesses
- IT
- arts administration
- board-level executives
- career development
- people management
- coach's coach
- team coach
- trainer's coach
- business coach
- vision coach
- relationship coach
- project coach
- call centre coach.

Additionally, I have recently come across a coach who specialises in acculturation (helping people relocate overseas). At the Aurora network meeting on coaching, mentioned above, the people present spoke of the following:

- a partner (at PwC) who works three days a week and has two coaches, an internal one and an external one
- a coaching exchange where coaches can go to be coached by others
- someone who specialises in coaching people who are not happy in their work.

This is by no means an exhaustive list of the specialties that there are or that are possible, but it bears out Stone's view of increasing specialisation among coaches.

I recommend to all coaches to identify your key specialty or specialties. Identify the top three and set out three reasons each one appeals so much and three reasons you are qualified to have this as your specialty.

I also recommend to all coaches to draw up a profile of your ideal client. For instance, identify your ideal client's:

- role in the organisation
- level in the organisation

- needs
- wants
- education
- lifestyle
- qualities
- dreams
- problems
- stresses.

Analysing your ideal client in this way will help you clarify the type of personality you coach best and the situation you coach best in. It will also help you put yourself across to the client to whom you are best suited. You do not need to restrict yourself to one ideal profile, but may have two or three.

HOW POPULAR IS COACHING IN EUROPE?

In making predictions about the future of coaching, it is interesting to cast an eye over the scene in the rest of Europe, where there are signs that coaching is gaining ground.

Silvia Guarnieri, a recent graduate in coaching based in Milan, has been researching into coaching in Italy and has also looked into its popularity in other European countries. Guarnieri has spoken to coaches in Ireland, France, Belgium, Germany, Norway, Sweden, Finland and Denmark, as well as Italy. Reports from these coaches indicate that around 20 to 35 per cent of organisations arrange coaching for their staff. By and large, businesses tend to view coaching as remedial, but there are signs that attitudes are changing. Indeed, we have seen an example in this book of the Italian Enel Group, where coaching is used as a high-impact development tool.

As might be expected, most international organisations, especially those that are American-owned, use coaching as a development tool in their European offices. As regards the coaching process and how this is implemented in Europe, Guarnieri found that most European coaches are using non-directive styles of coaching, and their philosophy is to work in partnership with the individual being coached to explore new possibilities and challenges together. Guarnieri concludes from her research that 'it is safe to predict that coaching will continue to gain in popularity in Europe and will be increasingly used for developmental and not just remedial purposes'.

A 1998 survey into mentoring conducted by John Walton found that mentoring was well established in Scandinavia – especially Sweden – and there were a number of examples of innovative practice.[3] However, he came across little evidence of mentoring in southern European countries, though he did detect a shift of emphasis away from a trainer-centred approach to learning and towards a more learner-centred one.

This shift in emphasis lends further weight to the prediction that the use of coaching is likely to increase in Europe. If this is the case, it will be important to bear in mind that coaching programmes from the US/UK may not travel well to a different European culture. Individuals and businesses seeking to introduce coaching initiatives in continental Europe must take into account the complex interactions of norms, beliefs, values and attitudes that distinguish one cultural group from another.

The growth of coaching in Europe is also giving rise to an increasing trend towards the formation of international and/or European networks. A number of these already exist, where coaches from different countries have formed an association to support one another, refer business, share expertise and coach one another. Networks are likely to grow as coaching gains ground internationally.

NOT A PASSING FASHION

Finally, let us re-emphasise the growth in coaching in the UK. An article in the *Harvard Business Review* in June 2002[4] suggests that there are at least 10,000 coaches working for businesses today in the US, and this figure is expected to exceed 50,000 in the next five years. While similar figures for the UK are not available, it is clear that executive coaching is burgeoning, and I estimate a similar increase in the UK over the coming five years.

This is not a passing fashion: I believe that the reason for this massive increase in the use of coaching is that it is a process and a solution, as I said at the start of this chapter, that suits our times. It is an effective mechanism for enabling an organisation to meet competitive pressures, plan for succession and bring about change. It is, above all, an effective and generally pleasant way for people to learn, grow and develop – to the benefit of themselves and their organisations.

NOTES AND REFERENCES

1   AURORA NETWORK MEETING (2002) Coaching Mentoring and Shadowing. May.

2   Corporate coaching teleforum (2003). www.impact-coaching.co.uk. 27 January.

3   WALTON J. (1998) *Mentoring in mainland Europe and the Republic of Ireland.* Herts, Herts TEC.

4   BERGLAS S. (2002) 'The very real dangers of executive coaching' *Harvard Business Review.* June.

Appendix 1

Received wisdom on e-learning

- E-learning should be regarded as a change initiative. It should not be seen as a way of making short-term savings.

- E-learning has to be driven by training, not technology. Training experts need to have faith in their own knowledge.

- There is a choice to be made between, on the one hand, introducing e-learning as part of a significant shift in the approach to learning and, on the other, proceeding through a controlled pilot project.

- The proportion of staff who regularly use a computer at work is a critical factor to be considered in the design of any e-learning initiative. The sophistication of these computers and any restrictions on their use must also be taken into consideration.

- Appropriate strategies must be developed for employees who do not have access to computers or the necessary skills to use them. The European Computer Driving Licence (ECDL) is receiving considerable attention in this context.

- There may be merit in making an open facility for staff (and their families) to access e-learning, but this should be undertaken to demonstrate a commitment to learning rather than a way of gaining immediate business benefits.

- Blended learning is seen by many as a process in which appropriate e-learning modules are a precursor to a training session in the classroom.

- The purchase of generic off-the-shelf material is most likely to be of value for IT end-users or in IT specialist applications.

- Generic soft-skills material will require careful selection and quality checks to test its relevance and appropriateness for the organisation. Even then it may be most effective in a blended solution involving face-to-face training.

- There is considerable interest in the generation of bespoke or customised material – either in-house through the use of an authoring system or by commissioning it from a specialist software supplier. Ease of updating this content is essential. Monitoring of usage is also a critical factor.

- Bespoke material is often first created to meet essential business needs (compulsory training). Other popular choices for the early use of bespoke material are performance appraisal, standard procedures or induction.

- Learners should be given the opportunity to carry out a learning programme in chunks of time that suit them. Some people may like to work in a concentrated manner and complete a whole programme at one sitting, while others may wish to complete the programme over several sessions.

- Online learning is more easily accepted in a culture of trust and empowerment, rather than in a culture where managers react against the idea of people being allowed to organise their own time and work schedules.

- Smaller organisations should enter into partnership over the running of online learning programmes so as to achieve maximum economies of scale and other benefits.

- Learning resource centres are seen as a useful facility, especially where a significant number of employees do not regularly use a personal computer at work.

- If a learning resource centre is intended to serve a population that includes those who are not regular users of personal computers, on-site facilitation is essential.

Reproduced with kind permission of the CIPD: SLOMAN M. *and* ROLPH J. (2003) *E-learning: the learning curve*. London, CIPD

Appendix 2

Biographical sketch form

Name:

Age:

Gender:

Marital Status (if children, how many, what ages?):

Current position/title:

How many people report to you directly?

Describe your current responsibilities:

What do enjoy most about your job?

What do you enjoy least?

What frustrates you most in your role?

What are the top three challenges for you in your current role?

What would you say are your three greatest strengths and weakness?

How would your friends describe you?

If you could change one thing at work to make your role more fulfilling, what would it be?

What did you do in your last two positions (job title/organisation, dates in position, brief description of responsibilities)?

What was a weakness at an earlier age that you've developed or become better at over the years?

What are the values that drive you?

How satisfied are you with your work on a scale of 1–10 (10 being very satisfied)?

What would it take to get to 10?

How many hours per day, on average, do you work?

What hobbies do you enjoy?

Thanks to Mike Travis, executive coach, USA for giving permission to publish this example of a pre-coaching questionnaire.

Appendix 3

Evaluation of AMA mentoring scheme (2)
Cohort 2 – Relationships started spring 2001

Your answers will be treated confidentially

Name (optional): _____

Mentor/Mentee (delete as appropriate)

1 **How many face-to-face meetings have you had with your mentor/mentee to date?** ☐

2 **How frequently do you meet with your mentor/mentee?**

☐ Once a month

☐ Once every two months

Other – please specify _____

3 **Have you communicated with your mentor/mentee by** (*please tick*)**:-**

Telephone   ☐

Fax   ☐

E-mail   ☐

Posted correspondence ☐

4 **How frequently do you communicate with your mentor/mentee on average?** (*Please tick*)

	Phone	Fax	E-mail	Post
Once a fortnight	☐	☐	☐	☐
Once a month	☐	☐	☐	☐
Once every two months	☐	☐	☐	☐
Less often	☐	☐	☐	☐
Never	☐	☐	☐	☐

5. **What, if any, difficulties have arisen over the course of your mentoring relationship?**
   (*Please list up to 3*)

   _____

   _____

   _____

6. **What are you getting out of your mentoring relationship?** (*Please list up to 3*)

   _____

   _____

   _____

7. **How could the AMA further support your mentoring relationship?**

   _____

   _____

   _____

   _____

As the mentoring scheme you are taking part in is a pilot for the AMA, any further comments you might like to make would be extremely valuable in informing future versions of the programme. If you have any other observations or remarks on this matter, please therefore write them below.

_____

_____

_____

_____

_____

_____

_____

Thank you for taking the time to complete this questionnaire. Do continue on separate sheets if you wish to give any other additional information.

PLEASE RETURN YOUR QUESTIONNAIRE BY FAX OR POST

With thanks to the Arts Marketing Association for giving permission to reproduce this material.

Appendix 4

Training in using a coaching style

The following are some examples of training modules used by different people. Details are also given of some exercises that are thought to be especially interesting.

A survey into coaching published by the Industrial Society in 1999 shows that the key components of coaching training, as used by the 339 organisations which took part in the survey, are:

Active listening 80%
Questioning 75%
Providing actionable feedback 72%
Facilitating 63%
Summarising 57%
Problem-solving 51%
Coaching models 50%
Philosophy of coaching 50%
Brainstorming 38%
Being directive 20%
Marketing suggestions 11%

MANAGEMENT SKILLS COACHING TRAINING

Coaching is about moving someone on so they know as much as you do. It is not telling them what to do. It is about giving people feedback and helping people identify their own solutions. It can be a corridor conversation. It involves a change in how the manager views their job. It is about being facilitative – not telling or demonstrating. It is about looking at your whole management style and looking at the organisational culture.

It is often a dilemma on a training course how to do the practical role-playing. Coaching people to draw a flower or stand up without putting their hands on the floor are fun but often unsatisfactory. It is preferable, therefore, to set up exercises in which delegates coach one another on business issues, perhaps with the course leader demonstrating the techniques first.

The following is a three-part training programme developed by Scala Associates for a local authority. The coaching skills are spread out over the three parts to give delegates time to develop the basic skills of active listening, motivation and giving feedback before moving to the deeper skill requirements of asking naïve or good-inquiry questions, and of learning to back off and not tell but facilitate.

LEADERSHIP SKILLS
MODULE 1: MANAGING PEOPLE

Objectives and key learning points

This is the first module of a three-part programme. The overall purpose is to equip managers with the skills required to lead and manage people in today's organisation.

By the end of this first module, delegates will have acquired techniques and skills that they can apply to a range of people-management situations.

This will include:

- awareness of different interpersonal and leadership styles, and how to adapt one's style to suit other people and different circumstances
- understanding how to develop the skills and techniques required to motivate others and delegate work.

Each module will be designed to build on the skills and techniques acquired on the previous module. One-to-one coaching, online support and e-learning exercises will be made available to delegates between each module.

Outline of course content

- Collaborative leadership model
- Active listening
- Understanding different interpersonal styles
- Motivation
- Situational leadership
- Delegation
- Giving and receiving feedback

Special points of delivery

Research shows that the most effective leaders and managers have a high degree of awareness of how their behaviour affects others. Once this awareness has been developed, individuals are then able to understand how they might adapt their behaviour to suit different individuals and different circumstances.

This workshop will include two behavioural models developed through self-awareness inventories: one on personal styles (Strengths Deployment Inventory) and one on leadership styles. (Situational Leadership). These inventories are non-threatening, as there is no one way that is better or worse, right or wrong.

Pre- and post-course briefings

Together with their immediate superiors, delegates complete specially designed pre-course briefings which will identify their training priorities. Post-course briefings are designed to aid discussion between delegate and line manager on how to implement the learning and to identify further areas of learning and development.

Number of delegates

A maximum of 12 delegates for each module.

Duration

Two days.

LEADERSHIP SKILLS

MODULE 2: HELPING PEOPLE GIVE OF THEIR BEST

Objectives and key learning points

This is the second module of a three-part programme. The overall purpose is to equip managers with the skills required to lead and manage people in today's organisation.

By the end of this second module, delegates will have built on the skills learned in the first module and will understand how a 'coaching style' of management helps people perform and develop. Delegates will practise the key skills of coaching and giving feedback. Delegates will also learn how to ensure that communication within their departments is effective.

This will include:

- Understanding people's different learning styles
- Acquiring and applying coaching skills
- Developing a common understanding of how to make performance appraisal effective and motivating.

Each module will be designed to build on the skills and techniques acquired on the previous module. One-to-one coaching, online support and e-learning exercises will be made available to delegates between each module.

Outline of course content

- Learning styles
- Coaching skills models and techniques
- Coaching skills exercises and case study
- The benefits of giving feedback on performance in 'real time'
- Giving and receiving feedback

- The importance of positive feedback
- Setting objectives and performance measures

Special points of delivery

This module will include one self-awareness inventory on learning styles. It will also include role-playing and case studies, as well as discussion.

PRE- AND POST-COURSE BRIEFINGS

Together with their immediate superiors, delegates complete specially designed pre-course briefings which will identify their training priorities. Post-course briefings are designed to aid discussion between delegate and line manager on how to implement the learning and to identify further areas of learning and development.

Number of delegates

A maximum of 12 delegates for each module.

Duration

Two days.

LEADERSHIP SKILLS

MODULE 3: CREATING THE RIGHT CULTURE

Objectives and key learning points

This is the third module of a three-part programme. The overall purpose is to equip managers with the skills required to lead and manage people in today's organisation.

By the end of this third module, delegates will have built on the skills learned in the first two modules and will identify how to create the right culture so as to ensure the Council achieves its aims of customer focus, teamwork and equality.

This will include:

- Understanding organisational culture
- Understanding that the key components to creating the right culture include using a coaching style of management, effective communication, understanding equality, managing change and team work. This will link into the exercises that delegates will have been working on between each module.

Each module will be designed to build on the skills and techniques acquired on the previous modules. One-to-one coaching, online support and e-learning exercises will be made available to delegates between each module.

At the end of this module, delegates will draw up action plans for transferring the learning to the workplace and career development plans.

Outline of course content

- Understanding organisational culture
- Identifying culture
- Effective teamwork
- Creating a team culture
- Managing change

Special points of delivery

This module will include one self-awareness inventory: 'the Belbin team roles' model. It will also include role-playing and case studies, a team-building game, drawing pictures and discussion.

PRE- AND POST-COURSE BRIEFINGS

Together with their immediate superiors, delegates complete specially designed pre-course briefings which will identify their training priorities. Post-course briefings are designed to aid discussion between delegate and line manager on how to implement the learning and to identify further areas of learning and development.

Number of delegates

A maximum of 12 delegates for each module.

Duration

Two days.

Bibliography

ALLEN K., BORDAS J *and* MATUSAK L. (1998) 'Leadership in the twenty – first century' *The Kellog Leadership Studies Project: Rethinking Leadership Working Papers*. Maryland, USA, Academy of Leadership Press.

ANDERSON M. C. (2001) *Executive Briefing: Case study on the return on investment of executive coaching*. Iowa, USA, MetrixGlobal. 2 November.

BERGLAS S. (2002) 'The very real dangers of executive coaching'. *Harvard Business Review*. June.

CARLING C. (2001) 'Reflections of a phone coach: does coaching by phone really work?' *Training Journal*. June.

CHAPMAN B. (2003) *LCMS Report: Comparative Analysis of Enterprise Learning Content Management Systems*. California, Brandon-Hall.com.

CHARTERED INSTITUTE OF PERSONNEL AND DEVELOPMENT (2002) *Who Learns at Work?* London, CIPD. March.

CHARTERED INSTITUTE OF PERSONNEL AND DEVELOPMENT *Workplace Learning in Europe*. London, CIPD. Available at: http://www.cipd.co.uk/infosource/conference.asp

CLUTTERBUCK D. (1998) *Learning Alliances*. London, CIPD.

CLUTTERBUCK D. *and* MEGGINSON D. (1999) *Mentoring Executives and Directors*. Oxford, Butterworth-Heinemann

CRIBBS G. (2002) 'The perils of choosing the right business coach'. *Financial Times*. 2 December.

DRISCOLL M. (2002) *Web-Based Training*. 2nd Ed. San Francisco, Jossey-Bass Pfeiffer.

GALLWAY T. (1974) *The Inner Game of Tennis*. New York, Random House.

GIBBS G. (1988) *Learning by Doing: A guide to teaching and learning methods*. London, FEU Longmans.

GOLDSMITH M. LYONS L. *and* FREAS. A (eds) (2000) *Coaching for Leadership*. San Francisco, Jossey-Bass Pfeiffer.

GOLEMAN D. (1996) *Emotional Intelligence*. London, Bloomsbury.

The HAY GROUP (2002) *The Future of Executive Coaching*. London, The Hay Group. Available at www.haygroup.co.uk

HERSEY P. BLANCHARD K. H. *and* JOHNSON D. E. (2000) *Management of Organisational Behaviour: Leading human resources*. 8th edn. New Jersey, Prentice Hall.

HONEY P. *and* MUMFORD A. (1983) *Using Your Learning Styles*. Maidenhead, Peter Honey Publications.

ICUS and HR Gateway.com (2002) *Majority of HR say e-learning a success,* ICUS London Availabe at: http://www.icus.net/media/PDF/Majority_HR_eL_success.pdf

KAPLAN R. S. *and* NORTON D. P. (1992) 'Putting the balanced scorecard to work'. *Harvard Business Review*. January-February.

KELLAWAY L. (2000) 'The life of a coach potato'. *Financial Times*. 14 February.

KELLERMAN B. (1998) 'The Kellogg Leadership Studies Project: Rethinking Leadership Working Papers' *The Kellogg Leadership Studies Project*. Maryland USA, Academy of Leadership Press.

KOLB D. *and* FRY R. (1975) *The Learning Circle of Experience*. Boston USA, McBer and Co.

LANDSBERG M. (1996) *The Tao of Coaching*. London, HarperCollins.

LORSCH J. W. *and* TIERNEY T. J. (2002) *Aligning the Stars*. Massachusetts, Harvard Business School Press.

MURPHY C. (2002) 'Careering towards a crisis?' *Director Magazine*. October.

PARSLOE E *and* WRAY M. (2000) *Coaching and Mentoring: Practical methods to improve learning*. London, Kogan Page.

PARSLOE E. (1999) *The Manager as Coach and Mentor*. 2nd edn. London, CIPD.

RANA E. (2002) 'What can we do to make it happen?' *People Management*. 16 May.

SCHEIN E. H. (1999) *The Corporate Culture Survival Guide*. San Francisco, Jossey-Bass.

SENGE P. (1990) *The Fifth Discipline: The art and practice of the learning organization*. New York, Doubleday.

SKIFFINGTON S. and ZEUS P. (1999) 'What is executive coaching?' *Management Today*. November.

SLOMAN M. (2001) *The E-Learning Revolution*. London, CIPD.

SLOMAN M. (2003) *Training in the Age of the Learner*. London, CIPD.

SLOMAN M. and TAYLOR J. (2002) *Customising the Learning Experience*. London, CIPD. April.

SLOMAN, M and ROLPH J. (2003) *E-learning the learning curve*. London, CIPD.

TULGAN B. (2001) *Winning the Talent Wars and Managing Generation X*. New York, Norton WW & Company.

VAN BUREN M. E. (2002) *State of the Industry: ASTD's Annual Review of Trends in Employer-Provided Training in the United States*. Virginia, American Society for Training and Development.

ZEUS P. and SKIFFINGTON S. (1999) 'The new coaching model'. *HR Monthly*. November.

Index